Sauntering Through Scripture

"This may be the most delightful journey through Scripture I have ever taken. Sr. Genevieve brings us right into the dusty sheep pens, windy olive groves, and starry, starry nights of ancient Palestine, and then, with great warmth and laser-like insight, offers us the kind of practical spiritual wisdom we have long been seeking and never will forget."

—Paula Huston, author of *One Ordinary Sunday:*
A Meditation on the Mystery of the Mass

"Sr. Genevieve Glen invites us to go on a walk with her as she ponders biblical passages and people, as well as prayers and psalms. What a marvelous expedition this is, filled with insights and challenges. Her beautiful and well-written reflections are poetic, engaging, and inspirational!"

—Robert F. Morneau, Auxiliary Bishop Emeritus
of the Diocese of Green Bay

"This gentle book encourages us to encounter the people and stories of the Bible in our own lives. Sr. Genevieve Glen has a gift for making us see even familiar stories with fresh eyes. As a monastic she is immersed in Scripture, day in and day out, and this book strikes me as one fruit of that life. Sr. Genevieve invites us all to share in the wisdom she's gleaned."

—Kathleen Norris, author of *The Cloister Walk*

Sauntering Through Scripture

A Book of Reflections

Genevieve Glen, OSB

A *Give Us This Day* Book

LITURGICAL PRESS

Collegeville, Minnesota

www.litpress.org

A *Give Us This Day* Book
published by Liturgical Press

Cover design by Amy Marc

Cover art: Shuoshu/Getty Images

Versions of many of these essays originally appeared in *Give Us This Day* (Collegeville, MN: Liturgical Press), www.giveusthisday.org. Used with permission. Several essays were adapted from the author's blog, *Take with You Words*, at genglen.blogspot.com. An earlier version of "Sarah: A Story" was published in *Pebbles on the Beach: Reflections for Lent and Holy Week* (Virginia Dale, CO: St. Walburga Press, 2009). An earlier version of "Salt Tears" was published in *On Threads of Hope* (Portland, OR: Oregon Catholic Press, 2008).

Excerpts from the English translation of *The Roman Missal, Third Edition* © 2010, International Commission on English in the Liturgy Corporation (ICEL); excerpts from *Order of Christian Funerals* © 1989, 1985, ICEL; excerpts from *The Liturgy of the Hours* © 1974, ICEL. All rights reserved.

Excerpt from the English translation of the *Magnificat* by the International Consultation on English Texts.

With the exception of psalms, all Scripture texts in this work are taken from the *New American Bible, revised edition* © 2010, 1991, 1986, 1970 Confraternity of Christian Doctrine, Washington, D.C. and are used by permission of the copyright owner. All Rights Reserved. No part of the New American Bible may be reproduced in any form without permission in writing from the copyright owner.

Unless otherwise noted, all psalms in this work are taken from *The Revised Grail Psalms*. Copyright © 2010, Conception Abbey/The Grail, admin. by GIA Publications, Inc., www.giamusic.com. All rights reserved.

3	4	5	6	7	8	9

Library of Congress Cataloging-in-Publication Data

Names: Glen, Genevieve, author.
Title: Sauntering through scripture : a book of reflections / Genevieve Glen, OSB.
Description: Collegeville, Minnesota : Liturgical Press, 2018.
Identifiers: LCCN 2018007313 (print) | LCCN 2018027486 (ebook) | ISBN
      9780814637258 (ebook) | ISBN 9780814637005
Subjects: LCSH: Bible—Meditations.
Classification: LCC BS491.5 (ebook) | LCC BS491.5 .G54 2018 (print) | DDC 242/.5—dc23
LC record available at https://lccn.loc.gov/2018007313

With deep gratitude to:

Mother Maria-Michael Newe, OSB, and the nuns of the Abbey of St. Walburga for all these years of a life saturated in Scripture, for your unfailing support, and for time and space in which to write;

Mother Marie André Campbell, PCPA, and the Poor Clares of Our Lady of Solitude Monastery, Tonopah, Arizona, for the hospitality of your prayer, silence, and friendship during part of this writing;

Peter Dwyer and Mary Stommes of Liturgical Press: Peter for the invitation to be part of *Give Us This Day*, that long-ago day at the Dairy Queen, and Mary, *editor extraordinaire* and friend. Thank you both for your constant encouragement, and for the keenness of your editorial eyes. Readers don't know how much they owe you—but I do!

And many thanks to all of you at Liturgical Press for your skill and hard work in turning manuscripts into books!

PRAYERS AND PSALMS

Introduction

Let's go for a walk. I know a place. So do you. It's a country rich in landscapes of all sorts. And it's as close as your Bible. As we travel through these pages, we find ourselves in a small village here, and there in a busy commercial town by the sea. Here there's a sandy corral full of noisy sheep and goats milling around, and there lies a green garden where the dead find a peaceful resting place. The long, dusty roads will take us to nomads' tents, beside pleasant waters, past fruitful fields and olive groves, and through a stand of sycamore trees. We will visit a stable, a rich man's house, a royal palace, and on more than one occasion, the great Temple in the city of Jerusalem. Of course, we will inevitably find our way into the desert, where God led the chosen people millennia ago and calls us still. We will even follow the path to the very edge of the world of time to see if we can catch a glimpse of what lies beyond it.

On this expedition, though, we are not searching out scenery for its own sake. We are exploring not the topography of Palestine and its neighbors but the landscapes of human experience that unfold there. Whether we encounter Palestinian villagers or an Idumean king's household, we will soon discover that whoever or wherever the original protagonists, the experiences are our own. You have read the Bible, so you know that already.

No matter where in those pages our travel takes us, everywhere we go, we will find stories and the people who inhabit them. The Scriptures offer us a rich gallery of characters both factual and fictional. As we saunter through, we will stop and shake hands with a few of them: Lot's wife, Martha and Mary, James and John, the rich young man, St. Lawrence of Rome. Wait!

St. Lawrence of Rome? How did he get in there? He lived— and died famously—in Rome, in the third century, long after the last pages of the New Testament had been written and the writers had laid down their styluses and quills. Truth be told, he arrived in my imagination one August 10, his liturgical feast day, wanting his story told, rather like a certain wizard boy who visited a then-unknown writer on an English train. St. Lawrence's story seems to read like an extension of the Gospels, so he seemed to fit with those who had gone before him. But the real reason he's here is that he insisted, and he deserved better than refusal. St. Lawrence is a fictional elaboration of a historical figure. I make no apologies. According to the literary scholars, the Scriptures offer us whole novellas centered on fictional characters: Jonah and Esther are well-known examples. And Jesus certainly makes up pithy short stories about characters like the woman who lost her coin and the barn builder, whom you will find in these pages. We call his stories parables, for so they are, but we often think and speak about their protagonists as if they had actually walked the roads of Palestine. The "prodigal son" seems as real to contemporary imagination as the kid next door who ran off with part of the family funds and wasted them all in clubs and fine restaurants and glitzy parties till hunger or remorse brought the wastrel home. So, near the end of the "People" section, when you come to a piece subtitled "A Story," "A Memoir," or "A Prose Poem," be warned: these are fictional vignettes spun around biblical characters or tales of the ones I call "the never-were," like the Palace Slave.

Biblical pilgrims must, of course, pray as we travel this land where all the ground is holy. The Scriptures provide us with a long-beloved prayer book in the psalter, but they have also inspired many later Christian prayers. You will find here a number of reflections on those prayers. You will also find reflections on some of the psalms themselves.

To a piece, these reflections are the fruit of my *lectio divina*, a centuries-old approach to the prayerful reading of Scripture.

I hope they will also support you in this ancient practice. Pope emeritus Benedict XVI, among others, has taught us the wisdom of *sauntering* through this land of Scripture—traveling slowly, booking no room for the night in advance, setting no deadline for arriving at journey's end. The word "saunter" means "walk leisurely with no apparent aim" or "to walk along in a slow and relaxed manner" or "to walk about in an idle or leisurely manner." Henry David Thoreau (1817–1862) offers an etymology that illuminates the title of this book, though it is no longer widely accepted. He says that pilgrims headed for the "Sainte Terre" (the Holy Land) came to be called "Sainte-Terrers" or "saunterers." A second etymology, also somewhat discredited, proposes a derivation from a Middle English word meaning "to muse" or "to wonder." Both capture the spirit of this little venture.

One last note: Scripture scholars have increased by leaps and bounds our insights into the texts we read and pray in our liturgical and personal lives. We know far more than we used to about how texts may have come into being, by whom and for whom they may have been written, and why. We know better than we did the tricky decisions that confront translators. However, there comes a time when the scholars themselves would invite us to lay the work of archaeology, linguistics, and textual study aside in favor of simply reading and praying the histories and parables, the laws and the prayers just as they lie before us when we open the pages. Since this is a book of reflections, not of critical and informative studies, that is what I have chosen to do, enlightened, I hope, by the hard work of scholars but not, in these pages, continuing it.

So, let us go for a walk . . .

Passages

Before the Fire

Exodus 3:1-5

To someone living outside a monastery, the Benedictine commitment to stability might seem odd. Yet isn't stability a good state for everyone, no matter their vocation? Of course, but what Benedictines promise is stability of place. Those of us who live in monasteries promise to stay put there as the central locus of our monastic life. We may come and go, depending on the monastery's lifestyle, but we always remain members of this particular house.

Long before St. Benedict wrote his Rule, Moses stood as a primary figure of stability—with equal oddity when you consider it. Think about Moses' first encounter with God at Horeb. He catches sight of a bush burning without being toasted to cinders. Moses ambles over to take a look. God calls out to him from the heart of the bush: "Take off your shoes! The place where you're standing is holy ground!" (Exod 3:5). How strange! Do bare feet really show more reverence than sandaled ones? Most restaurants don't seem to think so: "No shirt, no shoes, no service." Islamic custom dictates taking off one's shoes to enter the mosque, but Christian churches are traditionally more concerned about covering up body parts than uncovering them. Why bare feet?

Whatever the original explanation of the story, we can see Moses' bare feet as a challenge to honesty and commitment. To allow a part of ourselves to be seen uncovered is to allow ourselves to be seen as we are, minus the masks and makeup. To take off our shoes, especially in a stony wilderness replete with nasty things like scorpions, is to make it impossible to run away. We accept a position of truthfulness, powerlessness, and stability on this holy ground, felt through the soles of our own bare feet.

Moses remained faithful to the commitment he made in taking off his shoes. Certainly, he put them back on again after a while. Certainly, he became a powerful leader. Certainly, he lived a nomadic life from that moment to the very end. But how could one constantly on the move be a model of stability? Quite simply, Moses lived all his life in unveiled truth before the Holy One in whose footsteps he traveled (Exod 34:34). He carried the center of his stability with him. Or rather, the center of his stability carried him (Deut 1:30-31). God traveled with the people always. And when God stopped, the people stopped and pitched their tents.

Geography is not the point, then. Stability of presence is. Wherever God goes, we go; wherever God stops, we stop. Wherever God is, the surrounding ground is holy, whether it looks holy to us or not. And not all holy ground lies outside us. In our spiritual lives, for example, we might not care for this style of liturgy, or that passage of Scripture, or this form of prayer. But if God is there for us, we had better be there for God—and take off our shoes, settle down, and feel the reality of the holiness that pervades this "place" through the soles of our naked and defenseless feet.

The Sinai wilderness was not, in Moses' day, the Sinai Hilton: it was wild, threatening, low on human comforts—and holy, once the bush burst into flames there.

Unzip that Tent!

Numbers 11:10; Psalm 106:25

The story is told of the Israelites camped in the desert. They have escaped from the slaveholders of Egypt. They have walked dry shod through the sea, with the water standing like walls to their left and to their right. They have been given water from a rock in the parched and parching wilderness. They have been fed daily with the mysterious manna—the word means "What is it?"—in a land that offers little food. Their response? "If only we had meat for food! We remember the fish we used to eat without cost in Egypt, the cucumbers, the melons, the leeks, the onions, and the garlic. But now we are famished; we have nothing to look forward to but this manna" (Num 11:4-6).

In fact, they started grumbling the day after they left Egypt, before ever they crossed the sea. Complaint became their daily chorus. The psalmist says of them: "They complained inside their tents, / and did not listen to the voice of the LORD" (Ps 106:25). I imagine them camped in their tents, in the dark, the tent flaps firmly zipped shut. (Anachronism is no bar to the imagination!) There they sit, day after day, muttering to themselves and to each other, breathing the stale air of their own laments, sweltering in the heat of the anger they seem to stoke up every morning and refuel all day with their complaints: "We're tired of this desert, we're tired of the sand getting into everything, we're tired of this boring old manna, we're tired of each other, and, what is more, O Lord, we're getting very tired of you! When are you going to get us out of here?" Their tragedy is that, when Moses does lead them to the borders of the Promised Land, they complain about that too: "Sure there are figs, sure there are pomegranates, sure there are those gorgeous grapes Caleb brought back, but there are *giants* in there!" And they refuse to go in (see Numbers 13–14).

As the psalmist says, they have not listened to the voice of the Lord, who has done nothing but take care of their every need in the most startling ways. How could they listen to the divine voice when they were so busy listening to themselves?

Unfortunately, that scenario is all too familiar. Think of some Christmas past, or some birthday or other gift-giving occasion. In how many homes we hear something like: "You made bread dressing! I wanted rice!" or "I only got an e-reader! I wanted a tablet!" or "This sweater is red! I wanted blue!" In our local paper shortly after Christmas, the cartoonist Lynn Johnston in her comic strip *For Better or For Worse* poked gentle fun at a young wife saying to a friend, "Sure I gave him some hints, Anne! I said—buy me something frivolous and expensive—something I can show off to my friends." And, in the final frame, "I was thinking suede coat—while he was thinking dishwasher." The cartoon was amusing. Real life grumblers aren't. Theirs are the voices of the spoiled children in us who have never grown up. Grumbling is one of those occasional vices that grows all too easily into a habit of mind.

The way out is simple. God says to Israel in distress: "Enlarge the space for your tent, spread out your tent cloths unsparingly; lengthen your ropes and make firm your pegs" (Isa 54:2). In other words, "Open up, make room, I'm bringing you more gifts, more possibilities, more riches than you could possibly imagine. But you've got to unzip that tent!"

Sometimes it takes a lot of help to unfasten the elaborate system of zippers, buttons, snaps, padlocks, cords, ropes, and chains with which we secure our suffocating safe zones. Other people can help. God will help. But no one helps without an invitation. After all, you never know when walls, or tent flaps, are guarded with motion lights and sirens. I usually discover, though, when I finally manage, with help, to unfasten the tent flaps—the things that close me into the small, dark, stale circle of my own hungry, thirsty, and angry self-interest—that the sun is shining, the air is clear, and the desert floor is littered with manna as far as the eye can see. The trick seems to be to start by letting in a little laughter. Laughter is the best air freshener I've ever found. I recommend especially the kind that comes in the can labeled, "Laugh at yourself."

The best long-term cure for a bad habit seems to be to cultivate its opposite. The real antidote to the habit of complaint, once you've got the tent flaps open, is to cultivate the habit of gratitude: "Gosh, what great rice dressing!" and "I LOVE this Kindle" and "This red sweater is gorgeous! Thanks!" Grumbling and gratitude can't coexist in the same tent or even the same desert. Love doesn't actually mean never having to say you're sorry, as a thousand parodies have pointed out since that unfortunate line appeared in Erich Segal's *Love Story*. Love seems rather to mean always wanting to say thank you.

In Our Town Tonight

Luke 2:4-7

S o very small, so woefully inauspicious, the beginnings of salvation. There they are, the shepherds trooping in from the fields, the magi traveling from the exotic East, and hosts of angels pouring through the skies to sing hosanna—for what? The shepherds had been told to look for a savior, the magi for a king, but all they found was a child, probably one of several born in Bethlehem around that time. The shepherds wondered, the magi paid homage, but in later years the villagers of Nazareth would shake their heads in disbelief and turn away—"A wonder worker? Him? He's just the carpenter's son" (see Matt 13:54-56). His family thought him crazy (Mark 3:21). Some of his followers thought him extravagant (Mark 14:4-5). The authorities thought him dangerous, not because he was the Son of God but because he thought he was, and said so, to others who thought he might be right. They executed him for it, a criminal among criminals. And that was that, they thought. No one special, just another failed messiah.

We still make that same mistake, sometimes, in our search for salvation, whatever that word means to us. We look for the prophet clothed in camel hair, hurling imprecations (e.g., Matt 3:4-11), or we wait for a voice that speaks in thunder from the top of a mountain (e.g., Exod 19:16-19), but we miss a simple question asked by a friend, a question that might have turned our lives around had we been paying attention. "Why are you so angry?" or maybe "Do you really have to work all the time?" or "Have you ever thought of . . . ?" We scan the heavens for a star to show us the road (Matt 2:2), but we pay no heed to a news report on the homeless in our town tonight. We expect a blinding light on the Damascus road (Acts 9:3-4), but we fail to see the small, clear illumination shed by a word on a Bible page or the look in a loved one's eyes. Nothing special, the question, the news report, the word, the look—just another interruption in the real business of getting somewhere in life.

Tonight we probably won't see a stream of shepherds heading for a local motel, or a strange band of pilgrims holding up freeway traffic as they follow a star. It's unlikely we'll hear choirs of angels in the sky over the house, or even over the church. But tonight we will hear the same quiet invitation that has been following us around, perhaps for years, tugging at our sleeve and asking simply, as it asked shepherds and magi and later disciples of all sorts, "Come. I have what you're looking for." Nothing extraordinary, just our incredibly patient and persistent God, focused tonight on a baby laid in a beat-up food trough in a long-ago town in a faraway place, but in reality everywhere. Even right there, where you're sitting. "Come."

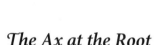

The Ax at the Root

Matthew 11:2-6; Luke 7:18-23

The Gospels recount a poignant "conversation" between John the Baptist and Jesus that invites us to look at the Gospel invitation to conversion.

The "conversation" does not take place face to face. John, already in prison, sends some of his followers to ask Jesus, "Are you the one who is to come, or should we look for another?" (Matt 11:3; Luke 7:19). Why John asks is anybody's guess. Some think he knew the answer but wanted his disciples to hear it for themselves. Some think John was genuinely puzzled: this Messiah was not the figure he had expected. That might be true. In Matthew 3:10, John threatens the Pharisees and Sadducees with a violent end: "Even now the ax lies at the root of the trees. Therefore every tree that does not bear good fruit will be cut down and thrown into the fire" (cf. also Luke 3:9). Maybe there's hope, if this "brood of vipers," as John calls them, finds the way into the baptismal waters under the Messiah's ministration, for the Messiah will baptize with fire as well as water (Matt 3:7, 11). But if they don't, this fearsome fire-bearer will sort them out accordingly: "His winnowing fan is in his hand. He will clear his threshing floor and gather his wheat into his barn, but the chaff he will burn with unquenchable fire" (Matt 3:12).

Along comes Jesus. No winnowing fan, no threshing floor, no fire-breathing prophet wearing a sign that says: "Your end is near." Instead, Jesus proclaims the good news of a kingdom governed by God's unwavering love and then gives a hint of what it will look like by making all sorts of broken human beings whole. We might well imagine that John would question whether this preacher and wonder-worker could indeed be the one he had promised would come after him.

Jesus' answer does not deny John's prophecy. It deepens it. Jesus tells the messengers, "Go and tell John what you hear and see: the blind regain their sight, the lame walk, lepers are cleansed, the deaf hear, the dead are raised, and the poor have the good news proclaimed to them." He adds, "And blessed is the one who takes no offense at me" (Matt 11:4-6). We can almost see Jesus looking over the heads of the messengers toward the faithful prophet hidden in his prison cell, wondering if he had wasted his breath and his life on a prediction that had failed to come true.

We can almost hear Jesus saying to this greatest of those born of women (Matt 11:11): "Don't worry, John. You had it right—you just didn't have the full picture. The ax does lie at the roots of the trees, but the trees are not Pharisees and Sadducees. The trees are that twisted, tormented growth born of a lie believed in a garden. The trees are all the harm wrought by sin and death among the beloved children of God. The ax—and I wield it—is already at work cutting down that growth at its roots. Ultimately, it will destroy the poisoned seed that has robbed my sisters and brothers of their ability to see reality as it is, to walk freely and without fear through the reign of God, to live together without biases or barriers, to discover that poverty may not be real poverty nor wealth real wealth. What you hear and see me doing is only a sign, real enough for now, of what I am really doing. I will destroy evil. I will destroy sin. I will destroy death. Oh yes, the ax is at work, and only the trees that bear good fruit will survive it. Don't be shocked that it is taking time. The roots are old and tough and deeply buried. And meanwhile, the blind, the lame, the lepers, the deaf, the bereaved, and the poor need what little I can do for them now so that they and all sufferers who come after them will believe the promise." One hopes John heard and understood the answer, and died satisfied with work well done.

That was then. Now we have seen what the ax was truly intended to accomplish. Now we have known the fire Jesus came to cast on the earth (Luke 12:49)—the fire that is God's living presence among us (cf. Exod 13:21). However, the work is not finished. The ax and the fire are still laboring to remove the ancient, evil-wrought undergrowth and leave the crop of righteousness and peace free to grow to harvest time (cf. Zech 8:12; 2 Cor 9:10, etc.). Now is always the time for pruning away all that hinders this healthy growth. The Gospel invites us to throw all the chaff—all those possessions, habits, thoughts, and activities that are empty and feed no one—into the consuming fire of God's forgiving love.

It would be a pity if it were we, and not Jesus, who left John's ardent hope disappointed after all.

Learner

Luke 2:52

W hat's in a name?" asks Juliet of Romeo.

In choosing names, biblical parents seem to have considered two options. A name chosen from the pool of relatives, apparently a common practice (see Luke 1:59-61), gave the child a family memory to live up to. But a name chosen by God often gave the child a purpose to grow into. "Jesus" did both. A name that sang memories of the Exodus: Joshua, another English form of the same name, served as Moses' apprentice, then led the people from the desert into the Promised Land. "God saves," the name meant in Hebrew, and through Joshua, God did. In Jesus, God would again save, but this time with a difference, as the angel explained to Joseph: "he will save his people from their sins" (Matt 1:21). "He," this child, not "God." Later scribes would object, "Who but God alone can forgive sins?" (Mark 2:6-7). Exactly, the angel might have said.

But Jesus did no forgiving until he went public thirty years later at the Jordan. In the meantime, back in Bethlehem, Egypt, Nazareth . . . what? The evangelists report messenger angels, startled parents, bewildered shepherds, and a handful of exotic strangers from the East, all with crucial information about the future of the Child whose birth we await during Advent and celebrate at Christmas. But what about the Child himself? Except for that one teenage venture into the temple, he seems to do precisely nothing worthy of note. Are we dealing with a thirty-year prologue to a sudden, intense story of salvation compressed into Jesus' three final years?

God is a better storyteller than that. Embryo and infant, toddler and teenager, the one about whom all that early fuss is made, does nothing—except what all children do from the womb to the grave: he learns. Admittedly, his learning has an edge to it: the one who had infinity and eternity for play-grounds now has to learn what it means to be constrained to one body, one time, one small geography, one circle of people. The one who is God's Word has to learn the complexities of vocabulary, syntax, metaphor. The one who is the *logos*, the principle of order in creation, has to learn how to wield hammer and saw. There is so much for a new human being to learn!

And Jesus does. Luke, in his last words about the young Jesus, hints at why this matters: "he advanced in wisdom" (Luke 2:52; see Isa 11:2). Now, wisdom is a lifelong learner in the school of experience. Wisdom pays attention, ponders, and makes sense of whatever life is handing out. And, learning, wisdom comes to understand.

"Understanding is a creative act in a dimension we do not see" (Elizabeth Goudge). Jesus' creative task was to rewrite the human story in the language of "yes" instead of "no." To do that, he first learned to understand *from the inside* what it means to be human. Understanding unfolds into love, the greatest of creative acts. Those private years of learning to understand and love made it possible for Jesus to work out the new story of salvation in the public years.

Jesus crosses the bridge from private to public at his baptism in the Jordan, the feast that concludes the Christmas season and marks our transition into Ordinary Time and beyond—learning, always learning. So much to learn!

Too Small

Micah 5:1-6; Matthew 2:1-12

Before germ theory put paid to the notion that if something is too small to see, it isn't there, before Silicon Valley discovered the magic of "micro," before the world learned that "small is beautiful," conventional wisdom held that bigger is usually better. From time immemorial, military strategy taught that it was better to be Goliath than David (ignoring, of course, the trouble a kid's slingshot, a small stone, and a shepherd boy had caused the Philistine giant). Defense theory maintained that to protect your country from hostile invasion, you could build a big wall—like Hadrian's Wall, 73 miles long, built in Roman times between England and Scotland; or the Great Wall of China, built over centuries across ancient China's northern border. Walls have been replaced now by intercontinental missiles and nuclear bombs, but the principle of building big is still in place. Bigger houses, bigger bank accounts, bigger yachts are still consumer ideals.

God seems never to have bought into the idea. The divine creativity made microbes, inspired microchips, and chose the shepherd boy for greatness (1 Sam 16). Although "least among the clans of Judah" was evidently the prevailing opinion of small Bethlehem-Ephrathah in the days of Micah, the prophet said on God's behalf that the little town of Bethlehem was the divine choice for the birth site of the Messiah (Mic 5:1-6).

When that time came, so did the Magi from the East, but either they thought the star they followed had made a navigational error or they simply gave no thought to Bethlehem over which it seems to have stopped. They headed straight for Jerusalem, a bit over six miles north of Bethlehem, where the reigning king's palace stood. It was a logical choice. They were looking for a newborn king after all. When they were redirected to the little town of Bethlehem by the chief priests and scribes that Herod consulted, they went without question. The evangelist does not record their reaction when they found the infant king in quarters much poorer than a palace and in the lap of a village girl. Matthew generously skips over that to the part where they recognized whom they were seeing despite the inauspicious surroundings and fell down in homage, laying their gifts, worthy of a king, at his mother's feet.

It's no surprise that the Child grew up to compare God's reign to a mustard seed and a handful of yeast. If you have ever seen a mustard seed, you know that it is in fact so small as to go unnoticed. Jesus may have been making use of hyperbole (a characteristic of parables to make a point) when he claimed the mustard seed grew into a tree. Mustard is generally a bush, but commentators have said that it was like the crab grass of Palestine. Once you let it start, there was no stopping it. It spread everywhere. Look at a map that shows the spread of Christianity after Jesus' resurrection. Crab grass indeed, as Roman authorities discovered when they tried to stamp it out!

Yeast is just as impressive in its own way, as you know if you have left a batch of bread rising too long and come back to find it taking over your kitchen. Or so it seems when you set yourself to getting the sticky stuff back under control!

Mustard seeds and yeast, village moms, and wandering bands of raggedy disciples make no noise. No fanfare announces them, no ticker tape parades welcome them, no red carpets unroll before their feet. They are too small, too insignificant for that kind of attention. The politicians ignore them. The crowds overlook them, trying to catch sight of royalty or celebrities riding down the street in limousines or elegant horse-drawn carriages.

We can understand the authorities of Jesus' day when they dismissed as unworthy of excitement the Child from the stable who had grown into a wandering young rabbi and later entered Jerusalem on a mere donkey, unheralded by trumpets and unaccompanied by an army in full parade dress. No, God never has bought into the notion that bigger or louder or flashier is better. Lucky for us!

Ordinary

Matthew 13:54-58; Mark 6:1-6; Luke 4:16-30

One day, Jesus went home to Nazareth. Perhaps he wanted to check on his mother. He had by then immersed himself in his public mission of preaching, teaching, healing, exorcising, and generally upsetting apple carts carefully filled with expectations of what is and is not possible, what could and could not be thought, what did and did not happen. His was a presence as often discomforting as it was comforting.

And so it proved at home. He went to the synagogue, as he always did, and he preached there, as he often had elsewhere. Perhaps in these early days of his ministry, he wanted to give the people among whom he had grown up the very best he had to offer: access to the kingdom of God. Jesus was no braggart with points to prove or grudges to settle. He loved his hearers and wanted what was best for them. So he gave them the best of good news.

You'd have thought they'd have been glad of it and maybe said thank you or invited him over for a meal or asked if he needed anything. Instead, they grumbled. They recognized his wisdom. They acknowledged his power to work wonders. And they didn't like it.

Perhaps it wasn't the wisdom and the power they resented as much as the fact that he had never, it seems, shown any signs of either one before. It sounds as if he and his family were people who had never given his neighbors any reason to take notice. That might seem odd to us, who pray to both of his parents and celebrate liturgical feasts in honor of the whole family. The most the Gospel suggests, though, is that their townsfolk had nothing bad to say about them. What they did say was that they were, well, ordinary. Certainly not a seedbed for raising a man suddenly noteworthy for his forceful preaching and wonder working.

And there's the rub. We don't like it much when the ordinary rises up and bites us with surprises. Storytellers have always exploited the dramatic possibilities of the day when the front door opens and the unexpected walks in. They might pique our desire to escape the humdrum, but honestly, most of us would just as soon that the schoolboy wizard or Sherlock Holmes would stick to the big screen or the pages of a book. We might enjoy visiting their world, but we'd usually like to come home to find our own intact. Catharsis via the vicarious experience of someone else's story has been recognized as the purpose of drama from the days of the ancient Greeks.

Apparently the people of Nazareth thought the same. They, like many of us, felt safer in a world where the carpenter's son remained a carpenter. He might be a dreamer, as the young Jesus is sometimes portrayed by later fiction, but his dreams should stay dreams and leave the rest of us alone in the comfort or even the discomfort of predictable reality. Or so they might have said.

No doubt their response grieved Jesus, who couldn't even heal their sick, except maybe for a few friends or neighbors who believed in him. Certainly it tempts present-day commentators to shake our heads at their disbelief and dismiss them as ignorant villagers, unaware of the salvation that had walked into their midst.

But don't we treat God much as they treat Jesus? We can recognize with awe the divine creativity in a spectacular sunset or a sudden glimpse of the Rocky Mountains. We can credit the divine inspiration behind a Beethoven symphony, a Shakespeare soliloquy, or an icon as piercing as it is mysterious. But God in ordinary dress? God tapping us on the shoulder through the next-door nuisance, or the to-do list hanging on the fridge door, or just the odd thoughts that sometimes float through our minds as we fall asleep at night?

No, let God alert us to the divine Presence in extraordinary beauty or extraordinary tragedy or extraordinary achievements, preferably accomplished by other people. But let God leave us alone in the ordinary rounds of an ordinary day when nothing really happens to trouble our expectations or our fears or our dreams. To be honest, the villagers might have said—and we might have agreed—Jesus is dangerous and should go and preach in Jerusalem where there are plenty of Pharisees and city sinners. But he should not bother us in the humdrum of our own daily routines or, most especially, in the privacy of our own minds. I like my apple cart full of untroubled memories and plans. Let the psalmists talk about God as an earthquake or a consuming fire. Let the likes of St. Paul get knocked to the ground by a blinding light. I'll keep my feet firmly on the ground, thank you. And, for that matter, I'd prefer the ground to stay firm too.

Be warned. Mary was minding her own business on a dusty village afternoon when the angel showed up, or so we can imagine (Luke 1:26-38). Joseph was brooding about a marriage contract and divorce when the angel interrupted his sleep (Matt 1:18-24). Jesus was born in an ordinary stable and laid in an ordinary manger, with no one troubled except a handful of unimportant shepherds in a nearby field (Luke 2:1-14). Jesus comes to us even now in ordinary human words printed on a page or spoken from the ambo. He even comes in disguise as something as down to earth as what looks like bread and wine, even though we try to fancy them up a bit for the purpose. The most dangerous place in the world is the ordinary when God gets hold of it. And God has.

The Logic of Paradox

Luke 14:28-33

For a wise teacher, Jesus seems sorely lacking in logic in this passage about calculating the resources available before you start an important project. He begins with a lesson in practical arithmetic with a sideways appeal to pride. To build a tower, like the small bell tower in my monastery's front yard, you first figure out how much it will cost, lest you run out of funds before it's finished. Any wise builder knows that. On another front, to win a war, you calculate the odds of pitting your army against one with twice as many troops. Is the landscape in your favor? Whose weaponry is greater? What tricks of strategy might swing the odds your way? Makes good sense. In neither case do you want to court ridicule if you fail.

"In the same way . . ." Jesus then continues, and we expect some similar logical advice about checking your resources if you want to be his disciple. But no. He tells us instead to jettison everything: "In the same way . . . every one of you who does not renounce all his possessions cannot be my disciple" (Luke 14:33). How's that for logic?

It reminds me, though, of the shepherd boy long ago (1 Samuel 17), sent to do battle with a formidable giant. King Saul rigs David out in all his own battle gear, the best to be had, only to find out the lad can barely walk. In the teeth of all convention, David sheds all the armor and weapons and goes to face his opponent armed only with five smooth stones, a slingshot, and faith in God. And both David and Goliath learn that those are enough.

Following David's lead, Jesus relies on the logic of paradox, which juxtaposes two opposites in a statement that turns out to be true. In this case, he says that the only resources you need to be a disciple are no resources at all, except sheer trust. It makes no sense. Until you realize that Jesus is describing his own armory.

The Company of Sinners

Matthew 9:10-11; Mark 2:16; Luke 5:29-32

Jesus kept company with sinners often enough for his detractors to point derogatory fingers. They made the charge frequently, but they never seemed to ask why. Jesus himself gave the reason: "to seek and to save what was lost" (Luke 19:10).

He meant it literally. First, he had to go looking for them, these beloved children of God who had somehow gone astray. Jesus found them everywhere: beside their fishing boats, in the synagogue, on sickbeds, and at the tables of Pharisees and tax collectors. But they did not everywhere welcome him. When the sinners made room for him at table and sat with him elbow to elbow, he was happy to join them, not to lecture them on their failings but surely first to listen to them. The evangelists rarely speak of Jesus as listening rather than speaking, but they show him over and over again to be a person who paid intense attention to the world around him, especially its human inhabitants and what went on in their hearts. One does not tell fascinating stories about people unless one has listened to them tell the stories themselves.

Listening leads to understanding, which novelist Elizabeth Goudge called "a creative act in a dimension we do not see." By listening to tax collectors and prostitutes and all the less spectacular sinners he met and ate with, Jesus slowly changed them. No longer the shamed scum the Pharisees and Sadducees thought them to be, these people could straighten their shoulders and walk a little taller because Jesus had taught them they were precious in his eyes and in the eyes of God. If that self-centered wastrel in the story of the prodigal son could be welcomed home (Luke 15:11-32), maybe they could too. Perhaps it was time to live up to Jesus' expectations rather than down to the expectations of the scornful finger-pointers. So, with Jesus' forgiveness and guidance, they did. We've been hearing their stories ever since, those sinners-made-saints in Jesus' company.

And their stories can be ours. The sharply pointed words of the prophets and psalmists often urge us to realize that "sinner" means "me." Uncomfortable? Of course. When I look in the mirror, I prefer to picture the saint and blot out the sinner looking back at me. With the ostrich, I believe that the sinner I can't see doesn't exist. (I wonder how many ostriches have suffocated out there with their heads in the sand.)

But if it's sinners Jesus likes to be with? If we want to find him, that's where we'd better look—at the sinners at home, in the next block, at work, on the news, in church. And in ourselves. Sit down with these beloved children of God. Listen to them. Learn their hopes and broken dreams, their fears and sorrows, the desires that reach higher than they—we—can. As Jesus taught, stop judging them, stop condemning them (Luke 6:37). Learn to understand them instead, really understand them.

Then perhaps we'll find ourselves at breakfast with Jesus, sitting on his side of the table. And realize that, faithless as we've sometimes been, he has been sitting there with us all along.

The Paralytic: A Portrait in Miniature

Matthew 9:1-8

It happened in Jesus' own town. Did he know them, the paralytic and his bearers? Did he know what burdens weighed the man down and pinned him to his bed?

Whether he did or not, when the friends presented the paralytic, Jesus saw beneath the surface of immobilized flesh and bone to the place where the man's real illness lay: his spirit. And Jesus healed that first, lifting from him the paralyzing weight of guilt by forgiving his sins.

No doubt the scribes had anticipated that he would heal the man. He had already cured crowds of the sick and the possessed, including a leper, a paralyzed servant, and Simon Peter's mother-in-law (Matthew 8). This time, he seemed initially not to heal the paralytic. Instead, he went to the heart of the matter: he first liberated the entangled spirit from whatever sins had bound the man to frozen helplessness. He knew that sin has real power: it can captivate, enslave, and paralyze the best of intentions and the strongest of wills. The scribes were appalled at the presumption of the claim he had made to have the authority to forgive. They knew very well that no one could forgive sins but God. Jesus knew it too. He made the claim again, but because he understood, as they did not, the layered depths of the struggle between the reign of sin and the reign of God, he translated his absolution into a word of cure. It seems almost an afterthought to the real healing. In the man laid before Jesus the paralysis of the limbs was a tragic icon of the paralysis of the heart.

Jesus was making no theological statement about cause and effect. In John 9:3, he repudiated the old Deuteronomic belief that all misfortune, including illness, is the product of sin, while prosperity is the fruit of righteousness. Job had long ago torn that theory up and thrown it to the whirlwind.

Personal sin is not the cause of every paralysis, but in every sickness, guilt over one's helplessness, dependence, anger, and despair can freeze what Viktor Frankl calls "the last of the human freedoms—to choose one's attitude in any given set of circumstances" (*Man's Search for Meaning*, 75). And self-centeredness is the dark whisper that tempts all of us in sickness and suffering. But the commandment to love God and neighbor without reserve has no exception clause for the sick and the sufferers. We see that embodied in Jesus himself during his passion.

In his helplessness, the paralytic is a portrait in miniature of the fallen human race. St. Paul captures the dilemma: "What I do, I do not understand. For I do not do what I want, but I do what I hate" (Rom 7:15). Jesus, the Word of God made flesh, cuts through the dithering that traps us in place: "Rise, pick up your stretcher, and go home" (Matt 9:6).

The Other Nine

Luke 17:12-19

When Jesus' contemporaries looked at a leper, they saw only danger. Some few, perhaps, also saw tragedy: "Oh that poor person! To be cut off from everyone and everything like that!" When Jesus looked at a leper, he saw the mother whose five children still cried for her at night, or the father whose family lived, barely, on the edge of starvation, with no one to bring home bread. He saw a face with a name, a story, an individual merely hidden by the sufferer's disfigurement. How could a personal God ever see less than persons? But Jesus saw even more. When he saw a leper he saw one more sign of evil at work: a person cast into the swamp of self-pity, fear, and despair that sucks the hopeless down into the dark, a family torn apart and bleeding, a neighborhood stalked by terror—who next? Me? Mine?

The power of the Spirit born in Jesus was called out to heal what had been brought to the verge of destruction by the mocking touch of the Enemy. Jesus gave all he had, one leper or ten. It didn't matter. Numbers were irrelevant in this struggle. Salvation is achieved one person at a time.

When he healed ten lepers he sent them to the priest to certify them clean so that their families and communities could take them home again. One stopped part way. Suddenly aware that he was whole again in every sense, he returned to offer the only sacrifice he could: his thanks, no doubt stammered with wonder. Jerusalem and Gerizim, the worship centers of Judaism and of the leper's native Samaria, became irrelevant: here was the Source of life, acknowledged and honored. The circle of Creator and created, broken by the Destroyer, was restored, the leper's commitment to God renewed. Jesus said so: "your faith has saved you."

Perhaps the man ran back to the temple for his certificate. Perhaps he just went home to Samaria, his smooth skin his testimonial to the work of God. The evangelists leave many stories unfinished, this one among them.

But what about the other nine? No doubt they did as Jesus had told them and went to the priests and offered the requisite sacrifices there. They had, after all, been made clean. And God—far less exclusive than the Pharisees or the Zebedee boys imagined (cf. Mark 9:38-41)—is hardly one to withdraw the healing because they didn't have the imagination to connect all the dots to Jesus and return to acknowledge him. The "connector" the nine seem not to have had is "faith in Jesus Christ and the One who sent him" (cf. John 5:24). It was that faith that gave the Samaritan the bigger picture.

Does that mean the nine were cured but not saved because they missed the hand of God at work in Jesus? Or perhaps they were not saved yet? Surely the cure, which they must have pondered deeply after the first euphoria passed, at least kept the door open?

But Luke does not say, and we are left to wonder. And to look to our own faith.

Sheep, Goats, and Shock Therapy

Matthew 25:31-46

Born left-handed, I get a little twitchy when I read the parable of the sheep and goats. Jesus assumes we know more than we do about the work habits of Palestinian shepherds. Why separate sheep from goats? His original hearers probably knew. But the story tricks the rest of us, in our twenty-first century ignorance, into assuming that the purpose is to sort the acceptable from those who don't make the cut. Sheep to the right, goats to the left, and you know which one you want to be when that roll is called up yonder.

It seems a little unfair. What makes a sheep better than a goat? The answer is: absolutely nothing, as far as I can tell. Genesis 1, where the business of distinctions and separations got started, cuts light from darkness, firmament from earth, land from sea, but makes no mention of sheep versus goats. Genesis 1:24 would lump them together as "tame animals," as opposed to wild animals and ground crawlers. However, not one of the seven days puts in place any hierarchy of "okay" and "not okay" among all these disparities. On the contrary, God pronounces it all good. So, God made both sheep and goats. The Israelites made use of both for their coats, hides, milk, and meat. No reason anywhere for the sheep to feel safer than the goats when judgment comes around.

In fact, for the listener, both sheep and goats turn out to be just woolly distractions from the main question, which concerns choices and consequences. The only distinction that counts in Jesus' parable is between the "doers" and the "didn't-doers." Both groups have one thing in common: their surprise. "When did we . . . ?" "When didn't we . . . ?"

I wonder if the reason they don't recognize what they have or haven't done is that they're both thinking too big. "I was hungry and you gave me food" could mean, as we often imagine, "I was on the streets, and you cooked for me at the soup kitchen (or didn't)." But it could also mean, "I needed a peanut butter sandwich after school, and you fixed me one without fussing (or you were too busy gossiping on the phone to fix it for me)." Or, "You knew how much I loved chocolate cake, and you baked one for my birthday and gave me an extra piece (or the next day you ate two pieces and left me none)."

"I was a stranger, and you welcomed me," could mean, "I was one of those tired, poor, huddled masses inscribed on the Statue of Liberty. Yearning to breathe free, I came across the Rio Grande, and you offered to teach me English (or you closed your neighborhood to me)." But it could also be, "I was the new kid in your class, and you smiled and asked my name (or you turned your back on me at recess)." Or, "I was the new hire at the office, and you showed me where supplies were kept (or you refused to show me where to get paper)."

The dramatic satisfies the imagination more than the everyday, but it's in the everyday where the commandments of love are mostly lived.

Whatever the details of what and when the sheep did and the goats didn't, Jesus intended the parable to serve as shock therapy to bounce us out of our complacency, especially our pious complacency. When we're tempted to stand at the front of the temple with the Pharisee in that other parable and read off the list of the religious good deeds we've done and demand the award we deserve, Jesus basically tells us we may have another think coming (see Luke 18:10-14). It's not that such things as prayer, almsgiving, and tithing don't matter. It's more that they're easier to fake, at least to ourselves, than spending time at the sickbed, or trying to understand the person imprisoned in a bottle of pills, or spending Sunday afternoon at the nursing home instead of the mall.

The deepest identity of the person at the receiving end (or neglecting end) of what we've done (or not done) may very well surprise us—but it shouldn't. Jesus says, "You did (or didn't do) it for *me*." We've had ample warning about the two destinations available when we reach the end of our story. Choose the action, choose the consequence: God has been trying desperately to teach us to grasp that equation since long before the first Scriptures hit the first piece of parchment.

All in all, I don't find any of the Gospel parables of the last judgment very consoling. I don't think they're meant to be. Jesus didn't tell them in order to pat complacency on the back. When I put this story of sheep and goats down, I want to beg the storyteller, "I didn't choose my dominant hand, but I can think of a few other choices I'd like to revise! Couldn't you put in one more chapter, one where I can at least make a stab at putting things right?"

Then I realize he has. Its title is "Right Now."

Finders Keepers

Luke 15:1-32

In Luke 15, Jesus treats us to a bit of parabolic rapid fire: the parables of the lost sheep, the lost coin, and the lost son hit us in quick succession. Those popular titles emphasize the lost, and rightly so from our perspective as hearers. We all know what it feels like to be the grubby lost sheep wandering far from pasture and shepherd's protective guidance; to be the lost coin gathering dust in a dark corner; to be the lost child hungering for hearth and home. But the three stories tell us as much about the finders as they do about the found.

Of course, Jesus doesn't say the parables are a self-portrait of the one who came "to seek and to save what was lost" (Luke 19:10). Parables are never so directly allegorical. But the Christian imagination finds it difficult to hear "once upon a time there was a shepherd" without thinking of Jesus, the Good Shepherd, a title Jesus himself claimed (John 10:14). Similarly, when we hear about a forgiving father, we can't help thinking of God the Father (even though the father in Luke's story never understood his eldest son and apparently didn't raise his youngest very well either).

Because we do hear these two echoes, we can begin to look to all three finders to teach us something about the actual work of forgiving sinners. Clearly Jesus is telling us that it's not merely a wave of the divine wand from a distant heaven.

Take the shepherd: this is a most attentive shepherd who notices that out of a very large flock of creatures that rarely stand still, one has gone missing. Off he goes, this almost careless shepherd, leaving ninety-nine to their own untrustworthy devices (we *are* talking about sheep here, those not-very-bright bundles of wool who spook easily and run off in every direction)—off he goes in search of just *one* lost sheep. Obviously it has strayed too far to get back under its own steam, so the shepherd—who has walked just as far or farther in his search—hoists it onto his own shoulders and carries it all the way back. Shades of a cross shouldered on that last dreadful walk up Calvary.

The parable of the lost sheep is a portrait of forgiveness that notices the need and doesn't sit at home waiting for sinners to drag themselves up and fall at its feet. This is forgiveness that that does not write the sinner off as a case of wicked perversity deserving nothing more than the fire. This forgiveness counts the sinner as one in need of retrieval—not a hope-less case at all. This forgiveness goes looking for the errant miscreant and works hard to bring him or her home. The sheep may wander off again, of course, looking for one more morsel of tasty grass. But if it does, it will very likely remember those strong shoulders, that journey home, and it won't add hope to the list of what has been lost. No wonder there's a big celebration in heaven when the sheep is brought back. The angels of the story know how much that homecoming costs.

The story of the lost coin repeats the same message in terms much more familiar to those of us who have never had the care of sheep, perhaps have never even seen one up close and personal. The woman who owns the coin works just as hard as the shepherd to rout out the lost tenth of her small store of money. Her story also hints at divine overtones, but perhaps more subtly. This "God-in-an-apron" begins very sensibly by shining a lamp into the dark spots where the errant coin may be lurking. Again, Jesus and his hearers know psalm verses like, "The LORD is my light and my salvation" (Ps 27:1) and "Your word is a lamp for my feet, / and a light for my path" (Ps 119:105). In this instance too, Jesus elsewhere claims the image for himself: "I am the light of the world" (John 8:12). Equipped with a light, the diligent housekeeper goes to work with a broom. You know how hard it is to track down a single coin, its gleam hidden under dust bunnies from the floor, when it has rolled under the couch! We can imagine the sweeper stirring up dust clouds, searching every corner, look-ing under every piece of furniture for that one lost coin. We can catch an echo of the Creator long ago wandering through the garden, looking for sinful human beings hiding in the bushes (Gen 3:8-9). And there is more.

In another story, in a debate with the Pharisees, Jesus him-self asks to see a coin used to pay the census tax. On seeing it, he asks, "Whose image is this? Oh, Caesar's you say? Then repay to Caesar what belongs to Caesar and to God what belongs to God" (Matt 22:16-22). Ancient Christian writers picked this up as an allusion to the fact that humanity was made in God's image (Gen 1:27). Perhaps that is why the parable's God-in-an-apron goes to such lengths to retrieve a single such coin. Here again, forgiveness has gone to work, hard work, to search out and retrieve the lost sinner, and is not afraid to get dirty in the process. And once again, heaven throws a party just for that one small lost coin found.

Sheep and coins, we know, can't make choices. Perhaps lost by their own devices, sheep still can't do anything but wait to be found. In the same way, a coin dropped and rolled under the furniture lies inert till it's retrieved. But the story of the lost son shows a very different face of forgiveness. Because here, we have a *human being*, a boy dazzled by the mirage of wine, women, and song, choosing to follow his own whim and taking off for the distant places where he imagines they can be found. There's no hint that he asked for his father's advice, still less his older brother's. He wanted to go, so he demanded his inheritance and went. The father, clearly anxious, doesn't go after him as the shepherd went after the lost sheep and the householder after the lost coin. He waits, keeping anxious watch for the wanderer's return, like King David above the city gate searching for any sign of his beloved but rebellious son Absalom's homecoming (2 Sam 18:24). David's moving grief for the boy who has wronged him so badly suggests how the father in the parable would react if he were to learn that his son had been truly lost for good.

Jesus and his hearers would have known David's story also. In the case of the prodigal son, though, the boy, his funds all squandered, finally comes to his senses and comes home, if only because he's really hungry. The father offers no reproach. He does not say, "I told you so." He doesn't lock him in his room on bread and water. Instead, he gives him an extravagant welcome: a feast, a splendid robe, a ring, and sandals for those travel-sore feet. In this story, forgiveness wears no frown of disappointment, makes no demands for a change of behavior, but shows only joyful relief and welcome to the lost one come home at last. Here the forgiving and prodigal parent, not the heavenly bystanders, throws the party.

A sheep, a coin, and a son. We can relate. But remember, always remember, the shepherd, the woman with the broom, and the parent. Nothing Jesus could have said about the redeeming love of a forgiving God could speak more vividly than these memorable sketches. Finders keepers? We have every reason to hope so!

By Pickaxe or Angel

Matthew 27:57–28:15

"The life of a monk ought to be a continuous Lent," St. Benedict says (*Rule of St. Benedict*, 49:1). If we usually consider just one Lenten season as an important but challenging stretch in our spiritual journey, how could we possibly commit to a lifetime of Lent? We might read the encouraging words of St. Benedict: "Do not be daunted immediately by fear and run away from the road that leads to salvation. It is bound to be narrow at the outset. But as we progress in this way of life and in faith, we shall run on the path of God's commandments, our hearts overflowing with the inexpressible delight of love" (*Rule of St. Benedict*, Prologue 48-49).

At least some of us have to admit that we don't seem to do much running. Sometimes an aging snail could beat us to the next turn in the road. At other times, we've spent most of our time picking ourselves up after falling over one rock in the road after another. The cautionary tale of Eve's conversation with the serpent in the Garden of Eden should alert us to the likelihood of stony patches on the road ahead (Gen 3:1-7). A more sober theological description would speak of the effects of original sin or the cumulative results of our personal histories of sinful choices, which do indeed hobble our feet or trip us up as we do our best to follow Christ, our Way. Some of these rocks are mere pebbles, easy to pick up and throw aside with a bit of repentance and some healthy asceticism to retrain our travel habits, but others loom large and immovable. At some point in our lives, we may even just sit down in the blocked path, put our heads in our hands, and lament, "How, O Lord, can this stone be uprooted? My pickaxe is broken, and I'm all out of dynamite!"

But every Lent ends with Easter, and the Easter story comes to our rescue with a hint and lesson. When Mary Magdalene and "the other Mary" arrived at the tomb that had been firmly sealed with a large slab of rock on Good Friday, "there was a great earthquake; for an angel of the Lord descended from heaven, approached, rolled back the stone, and sat upon it" (Matt 28:2).

Let's consider the purpose of that stone to begin with. It wasn't intended to keep Jesus in. It was meant to keep others out. As we learn from John's account of Easter evening, locked doors and stone walls didn't deter Jesus from coming into the room, so no gravestone would have barred his way (John 20:19). No doubt Joseph of Arimathea, who put the stone in place over the tomb in Matthew's account, wanted to preserve the dead Master from any indignity on the part of intruders. The chief priests and Pharisees were more worried about the disciples stealing the body and then claiming that Jesus had risen from the dead, so they demanded guards as well as the stone itself.

Sometimes, as we're sitting down before a large lump of stone in the path, it helps to remember the purpose of that stone too. It's meant to do just what it has done: to stop us in our tracks while Jesus disappears from sight down the road beyond it, or we imagine he does. The rock is meant to keep us away from joining him. It's interesting to wonder who put it there. It may look at first blush as if we did. If it's a weighty composite of our own history of selfish wrongdoing, yep, we made it. But in life as in Lent—in a life that is a "continuous Lent"—we set out with the intention of breaking through whatever keeps us from following the Lord. We surely wouldn't drop a boulder on the way to make that harder. The psalmists warn of traps, sometimes in the form of pits, laid across our path by an enemy (e.g., Ps 7:16; 35:7; 140:6; 141:9). This rock has trapped us. It's not unknown for the true Enemy to use our own weaknesses, failings, and sins as traps and pits to keep us from reaching our Easter destination. So who is most likely to have dropped this rock right in front of us to bring our "run" to a skidding halt and make us sit down in discouragement, thereby guaranteeing that we will go nowhere soon?

This is where the Easter angel of Matthew's story comes in. First, the angel presents us with the sobering truth that just as the tombstone was too heavy for the women to roll back, some rocks are indeed too formidable for our little pickaxes. Second, perhaps the angel makes clear the even more sobering truth that if we have imagined all along that rock removal, even pebble removal, was primarily our responsibility, it's about time we met reality face to face. One of life's hidden temptations is the illusion that we are our own saviors. We decide what our "Continuous Lenten" program will be: what sins and failings we will address, what our conversion will look like, and what steps we will take to engineer it. Sorry about that, the angel seems to say. It's true that you are an indispensable collaborator in the work, you and your little pickaxe, even when you're tired of the effort, discouraged by apparently poor results, and ready to punch out on the conversion time clock. But you are *not* the primary force in blasting pebbles and mountains out of your way as you seek to run toward that great encounter we call Easter. That would be God, says the angel (who is, of course, God's messenger).

We all know that neither God nor our lives are confined by a liturgical calendar or season. The season of Lent ends, but the work of Lent never does. The rock on the road and the stone at the tomb, with the angel sitting atop it, are always there to remind us of the reality and power of God's grace, even when the Rocky Mountains themselves seem to have sprung up between us and the Lord we seek. As the women at the tomb learn from the angel, though not in so many words, it's really the Lord who is seeking us. And to God, even mountains are pebbles.

What the Tomb Proclaims

Matthew 28; Mark 16; Luke 24; John 20

On that first morning of the week, day breaks into chaos. Sorrow, joy, disbelief, and hope fight out rival claims to the disciples' hearts as rumors and stories chase one another through the community. No wonder the accounts clash! Amid the confusion, though, one irrefutable fact stands out: The tomb is open. And it is empty.

Explanations spring up like weeds. The ubiquitous "they" have carried Jesus off, says Mary Magdalene to a doubtlessly amused "gardener." Not any "they," claim the guards assigned to prevent that very thing. His own disciples stole the body away in the night, they say, their employers' bribe jingling in their pockets. But no, counter some of the women. He met us. He talked to us on the road. He's alive. As more and more voices add to their chorus, and tales of Jesus' appearances multiply, the tomb begins to fade into the background, and the witnesses move elsewhere.

But still the tomb stands open. And still it is empty.

The Church of the Holy Sepulcher in Jerusalem contains an empty spot venerated as its very site since the fourth century. But the point is not a place back then or over there somewhere. The point is the tomb's proclamation of Easter here and now.

From the Israelites in the desert to the Pharisees in Jerusalem, God has lamented our human habit of burying ourselves not in the ground but in the stone caskets of hardened hearts. God calls to us still today in Psalm 95, often prayed at the beginning of the Church's Morning Prayer: Don't do it again! "Harden not your hearts as at Meribah, / as on that day at Massah in the desert . . ." when Israel, fresh out of Egypt, refused to trust that God would do anything about the hunger and thirst that were killing them (Ps 95:8-9). They could not imagine that God would summon a future for them out of the desert wastelands, even though they had seen the sea open at their feet (Exod 14:21-22). And where imagination is locked in a box, hope suffocates and dies.

In the Gospels, Jesus grieves over the Pharisees. Their hearts have hardened into whitewashed sepulchers, filled with the bones of their dead forebears' hopes (Matt 23:27). The prophets had fueled those hopes with the promise of a new covenant. Its laws would be written not on stone tablets but in human hearts (Jer 31:33). But the Pharisees have shut their eyes, ears, and hearts to any possibility that God might break out of their own stone-carved rules, even when the new law-made-flesh in their midst raises the dead to life before their very eyes.

We know them, the Israelites and the Pharisees. We know what it is to seal ourselves into stubborn refusal of Christ's invitation to come out of the habits of mind and spirit that are slowly destroying us. We are afraid, as the disciples were afraid behind their locked doors on Easter night (John 20:19). We dare not hope any more than they did that God will overcome the invisible enemies threatening us with suffering and death.

The tomb still stands open. And it is empty. It announces that no tomb can hold us now, not even our self-made sepulchers, unless we choose to stay. When our imagination fails and hope withers, the tomb proclaims in silent boldness that all things are possible with God.

Alleluia!

The Bifröst

Luke 18:8

In the 2011 movie *Thor*, the legendary Norse god of thunder and lightning and protector of earth, is translated from a divine being into a contemporary superhero deeply committed to the safety of our small, troubled planet. Thor lives in the distant world of Asgard, separated from earth by the "bifröst." In Icelandic legend, the bifröst is a burning rainbow bridge. In the movie, it starts out as beautiful bits of rainbow encased in a clear glasslike solid, and then it becomes a powerful rainbow-colored stream of pure force capable of transferring Thor and his companions to our world at high speed. During the movie, circumstances force Thor to destroy it, thus cutting off his only path to his beloved earth. In a poignant moment near the end of the film he stands looking out over the edge of the broken bridge and asks the bifröst's guardian, "So earth is lost to us?"

The moment reminds me of Jesus' equally poignant question, "When the Son of Man comes, will he find faith on earth?" (Luke 18:8). Faith—understood both as "trust in" and "belief that"—appears in the Gospels as the essential bridge that allows Jesus to reach the depths of people's hearts and there work wonders of transformation. Recall his return to Nazareth where his former neighbors remember him well as the village carpenter, son of the carpenter Joseph and his wife Mary. Indeed, so well do they remember him as the ordinary son from an ordinary family that they cannot stretch their minds further. They can't possibly take in what Jesus is trying to tell them about his real identity and mission: he is the one of whom Isaiah prophesied, the one chosen and sent as the bearer of God's Spirit. ("Good grief! Is he claiming to be the Messiah? He's just the kid next door!" you can hear them whisper.) His task now, he tells them, is to translate the good news that God's reign has come into real human experiences of healing and liberation from evil's oppression. But they just can't make that leap. The evangelists call their failure of imaginative nerve a "lack of faith." And that lack, they say, prevents Jesus from working "mighty deeds" in their midst (Mark 6:1-6; Matt 13:54-58; Luke 4:16-30).

And think how often Jesus says to someone he has just healed or freed of demons, "Your faith has saved you." There is the woman with the hemorrhage, desperate after years of failed medical treatments but healed after simply touching Jesus' clothes because she believes (Mark 5:25-34). There is the blind beggar Bartimaeus who pesters loudly enough to get Jesus' attention despite all efforts to hush him. He even throws off his cloak to get there faster when Jesus calls him. Jesus tells him too, "Go your way; your faith has saved you" (Mark 10:46-52). The need for healing is not always physical. There is the sinful woman who gatecrashes the Pharisee's dinner party to perform an extravagant ritual of repentance and gratitude. Jesus tells her that her sins are forgiven, for her faith has saved her (Luke 7:36-50).

But the story goes even further back, to the incarnation. As St. Augustine said in the fourth century, Mary conceived Jesus *in faith* before she conceived him in her womb. Other early Christian thinkers joined him in a chorus of grateful praise of the Virgin's faith, for that is what gave the Word access to become flesh for our salvation. There at the very beginning of the story, Mary's faith served as the bridge across which the Savior entered human history.

When Thor asked if earth was lost, the bifröst's guardian replied, "No, there is always hope." When Jesus asked if faith, his bridge, would still be there when he comes again, there was no one to answer. But much later, the author of the Letter to the Ephesians prayed for all future believers, including us: "that Christ may dwell in your hearts through faith" (Eph 3:17). If we allow him to, then there is indeed hope that when Christ comes again the bifröst will indeed be open.

Long-Fingered Light

Matthew 28; Mark 16; Luke 24; John 20

Easter lies too far beyond our experience for us to grasp more than impressions of startling appearances by a Jesus who is but isn't dead, is but isn't a ghost, is but isn't the familiar figure his followers knew so well. What was he like? Well, flesh but not flesh as we know it, wounded but not with wounds as we know them, transformed but not in any way we can really picture. He appears unannounced in locked rooms, walks incognito with discouraged disciples, eats solid food but passes through solid walls. Conceptual explanations of the resurrection don't help much more than our flawed images do. They make use of words we know, but they use them to expound a reality we don't, not really.

We're in good company, to judge by the general confusion that seems to have left the first Christians babbling contradictory accounts of who saw what when and who believed whom—or didn't. A stammer was probably the most honest way for them to describe a reality into and over which they stumbled in happy but fearful discovery. Perhaps our own Easter alleluias are our contemporary way of stammering out a truth for which we have no coherent words.

The risen Christ, transformed into the Fire hidden at the heart of human flesh, sheds a light so bright it blinds us. Paul discovered that on the Damascus road (Acts 9:1-9). But he was not the first to learn it. Jesus' resurrection appearances are stories of that light reaching out to touch one by one the dark places in which his early followers walked: the apostles' fear, Mary Magdalene's grief, Thomas's angry doubt, Peter's shame. Those stories console because the beloved Christ appears in person to cast light into murky experiences we too have known. Fear, grief, doubt, and shame are shadows through which we have all walked.

But the story doesn't end with those personal post-resurrection encounters. Jesus disappears from the scene at the Ascension, or seems to, but the Light does not. In the Acts of the Apostles we see a lame man, condemned to a lifetime of begging, spring up and walk at the sound of Jesus' name (Acts 3:1-10). We recoil at an angry mob stoning Stephen, but Jesus appears to him in glory (Acts 6:54-60). We hear of disagreements between Christians of differing ethnic origins settled by Peter's creative wisdom (Acts 6:1-7). We see disciples jailed (Acts 4–5), apostles arguing policy (Acts 15:1-21), missionaries thrown out of town (Acts 14:11-19), communities split (1 Cor 1:10-17). We see, in other words, all the dark corners in which Christians sometimes find themselves even now, some two millennia after the resurrection. The darkness of the New Testament Church is far from outdated.

In Acts, we do not see Jesus appearing to solve the problems, at least not as he did in the Gospels. Instead we see what he promised: the power of Spirit and Word working to enlighten flawed human beings to see things in new ways, to discover what it really means to "love your enemies as yourself," to pick up pieces and put them back together in innovative ways so that the image of God can shine more clearly in a world still deeply held in the grip of night.

The Light still reaches long fingers from God's hidden depths into our present shadows. I cannot really imagine the risen Christ. All my inner pictures seem unreal. But in the annals of the early Church, in the chronicle of the world, and indeed in the story of my own soul, I can see the Light at work. And that Light is very real indeed.

Ghost

Luke 24:36-37

While they were still speaking about this, he stood in their midst and said to them, "Peace be with you." But they were startled and terrified and thought that they were seeing a ghost.

What is a ghost but memory made wispy flesh?

They have good reason to fear this memory, the disciples. It comes to them clad in grief and guilt—their grief, their guilt, not his. They believed in him, or thought they did. They loved him, or thought they did. They left a lot behind to follow him. Then they left him. Terror pierces through the grief and guilt. Will their abandoned families take them back? Will their villages look at them with anything but suspicion, scorn, maybe pity if they're lucky? Are boats and nets and tax collector's booth still waiting, or has someone else taken them over? There they are in the upper room, the crumbs of the supper still on the floor, and they locked into an empty limbo, unable to go back, afraid to go forward.

And suddenly there he is, the reason for it all. They hope he is a ghost, mere memory made wispy flesh. He will haunt them all their days in any case, this man—surely no more than that? He died, after all, whatever he may have seemed to claim or promise. But . . . he will haunt them, clad in their grief and guilt, this man they believed in and loved and left before he could leave them. But you can live with ghosts and go about your business. The hardy reality of wives and mothers-in-law

and children demanding to be fed, of nets and boats and clink-
ing coins will hold the ghosts at bay until they fade. Except
maybe at night when all the others are asleep and you're not.

And here he is, ghost and nightmare, absolving them with
a word: "Peace." Well, he had always seen right through their
blustering and swaggering to their fears and griefs and guilt.
Perhaps they begin at this moment to allow a tiny fragile shoot
of hope to break through the stone walls of their prison, their
tomb.

Then he clinches it. He forces them to face the truth from
which they're hiding. He never has allowed evasion. Always
truth with him. He makes them look at his hands and feet,
touch them even. He makes them confront the fact of his
wounds. They weren't there to see him get them, you see, except John. Now he makes them face the thing they fled. The
world-shattering reality of the cross, and of him hanging on
it, beaten, bruised, bloody, dying, dead. It is not his strength
he reveals to them there in that upper room. They have already
seen and believed in that: the blind wondering at the sunlight,
the deaf hearing their children's voices, a seemingly dead girl
hugging her mother and eating a bit of bread. It is not his
strength they are forced to own now, but his weakness, which
is theirs, his wounds, which are theirs, his mortality, which is
theirs. Weakness not denied but accepted as the only source
of strength for them. Wounds not refused but held open as
the only source of healing for them. Mortality not rejected but
embraced as the only source of life for them.

At last they know him for what he really is.

And they are us.

People

The Call of St. Matthew: A New Creation

Matthew 9:9-13

What readied the tax collector to abandon his post at Jesus' call? The Gospel does not say. Experience suggests that something must have given him itchy feet: a restlessness, a dissatisfaction, a sense that life at the tax office lacked sufficient purpose. Coins in one's pocket have a nice jingle, but they hardly weigh in among the greathearted reasons for living. As a measure of life's fruitfulness, they are a dead crop.

Fruitlessness is characteristic of the primal chaos described in Genesis 1:2, where the world is said to be "without form and void." The Hebrew words mean "emptiness" or "futility," like a desert. Nothing grows there. It is useless. If Matthew thought his life had become pointless, he was ready for a change.

But the primal chaos was not nothingness. It was possibility. God looked upon it with love, that is, the will to bring it to its best. The formless void, the dark waters, proved to be in fact a seething cauldron of prospects awaiting only God's creative word to leap into actuality as sun, moon, stars, and all the rest of creation.

We can surely say that Jesus looked with love upon Matthew, sitting at his tax post, perhaps fretting for he knew not what. And Jesus spoke a new creative word: "Follow me" (Matt 9:9). The words did not simply invite Matthew to take a walk down the street behind Jesus. They invited him to become a disciple, one who moves in with a teacher, learns from the teacher, seeks to become a living image of the teacher. And that is the crux of this new little creation story, the call of Matthew. In Genesis, "God created mankind in his image," including in the one image both male and female (Gen 1:27). In the Gospel, Jesus called Matthew to become the image of the Caller, who is "the image of the invisible God" (Col 1:15).

As image of Jesus, Matthew had a new and all-consuming purpose. He was to do the Teacher's work in his own uniquely personal style. Just as Andrew, James, and John left nets and boats to become fishers in a different sea (cf. Matt 4:19), so Matthew left his tax table to trade with a livelier kind of gold. Tradition attaches his name to the first Gospel, which is characterized by Jesus' five long discourses. These words, treasured by believers down the centuries, are themselves creative "words of eternal life" (John 6:68). Matthew collected them and still scatters them freely in every corner of the world. Wherever they fall, they offer new possibilities, new purpose, new life. Golden words!

With, and sometimes through, Matthew, we too are called out of whatever sense of purposelessness and restlessness might be giving us itchy feet. We too are invited to follow Jesus—to become poor in spirit, hungry for justice, willing for persecution, eager for the Gospel. We too are invited to gather up the words of gold that have transformed us and scatter them abroad like seeds of a future harvest—to allow God's creative word of love to leap into actuality in and through us.

On the Brink: Zacchaeus

Luke 19:1-10

The twinkle in the storyteller's eye masks the enormity of the little tax collector's story. Small in stature he may have been, but he was a big man in town. Not just any tax booth staffer, but chief tax collector. And rich. Someone like that was no figure of fun. Tax collectors had the power to make demands that brooked no refusal. Wealthy ones did not grow fat on the milk of human kindness. One might fear a man like Zacchaeus or despise him. One did not laugh at him.

Yet he swarmed up a tree like an undignified monkey to get a look at Jesus passing by. What could so have burned his self-importance to a crisp? Why did he want so badly to see who this Galilean was? He had gotten where he was not by climbing up sycamores but by stepping on heads. And there he sat, feared and alone. At the top one has no peers, only victims, subordinates, and competitors. Did he want a way down without quite daring to admit it?

He obviously had some idea of Jesus' teachings. Did they hold some glimmer of promise for him? A glimmer scary enough to send him up a tree instead of to Jesus' feet, perhaps, but enough to make him seek something, even at a price he might not want to pay. He would certainly get more than he bargained for. From his treetop perch he teetered over a brink he couldn't see.

Jesus stopped beneath the tree and called him by name. He must have known the tax collector by reputation as well as by name, but he passed no judgments. He simply invited himself to stay at Zacchaeus's house.

That was when that mouthful of extravagant pledges fell over each other as they poured out: "half my possessions, four times what I've extorted." And Jesus replied with the same extravagance: "today salvation has come to this house." Not a thank-you note, not a polite bottle of wine, but salvation. And with a word, Jesus also restored this public sinner to the place he had long ago forfeited among Abraham's descendants. Jesus did not take lightly the dire state Zacchaeus had reached on his climb up the career ladder. The tax collector was truly lost. Now found, he was offered something far more lasting than gold. Salvation is not a coin to spend in a moment. It's a way of life that binds God and the believer together as partners in a great adventure.

The evangelist left Zacchaeus there, still on the brink of a bright new world, but life surely didn't. As all of us must, Zacchaeus eventually had to come down from his high and look the morning after in the eye. Jesus gone, the moneybags deflated, the publican's social status somewhere between grudging acceptance and lingering suspicion, his old ways behind him—what now?

That question follows relentlessly on the heels of every encounter with Jesus. You have met him in this Gospel story. So, what now?

A Daughter of Abraham

Luke 13:10-13

Her condition is plea enough for help. She makes no complaint. She asks for nothing at all. She simply stands there in the synagogue, on the Sabbath, where the word of God is read and expounded. It must be difficult for her to walk from home, but she comes anyway. She makes herself available to the word. That is all.

It is enough. Jesus sees her need. Her plight seems the kind of ugly irony that evil enjoys. Bent in two, she is a parody of a worshiper bowed down before God. Jesus speaks the word that cuts the unseen tie that has bound her, face to the ground, for eighteen years. "The word of God is . . . sharper than any two-edged sword" (Heb 4:12). At his word, the parody turns into truth: as soon as he frees her to stand up straight, she immediately glorifies God.

Perhaps that has been her inner truth all along. Jesus does not see any need to forgive her, as he sometimes forgives those who ask for healing. She has not withdrawn into bitter isolation. She has joined the community at prayer around God's word. She has remained what Jesus calls her, a "daughter of Abraham," a faithful and faith-filled member of the covenant community in service to the God of impossible promises and startling fulfillments. She gives no indication that she has ever expected to get anything out of it for herself.

She teaches us something about what it means to ask and receive (cf. Matt 7:7), this woman who says nothing, who merely stands before the word, her very reality an unspoken statement of need, but not a statement she herself draws any attention to. She puts to shame intercessory prayer that provides God with a complete and detailed description of what is needed, followed by painstaking instructions as to what should be done about it: "For my mother, who has suffered for eighteen years and thirty-three seconds from severe osteoporosis and arthritis that keep her from driving a car or running a vacuum cleaner, and that four doctors have been unable to help, though she has spent a fortune on medication; that she be able to stand up straight so that she can babysit the grandchildren on Tuesdays and Thursdays while their mother is at work, we pray to the Lord."

Jesus had things to say about multiplying words in prayer, including, "Don't" (Matt 6:7). "Your Father knows what you need before you ask him" (Matt 6:8), he said. And, "This is how you are to pray: Our Father"—prayer that captures all the essentials in very few words indeed (Matt 6:9). The woman in the synagogue needs no such instructions. Her need and her faith are her prayer. And Jesus hears them.

Barn Builder

Luke 12:13-21

When it comes to retirement planning, the farmer in this parable has it well in hand. He looks over the bountiful crops his fields have produced and perhaps the grapes hanging heavily on the vine and the olives weighing down the branches of the trees in the olive groves. Now there, says his experience, lies a handsome future indeed! Then there are his flocks, thick fleeces just waiting for the shearing. Pictures of the heavy bales dance in his head, along with the baskets of wheat and the wine skins and the jugs of olive oil, all doing the tango in his dreams.

One slight problem pokes at his waking thoughts. Those barns out there are just too small! What shall I do, he asks himself, as any of us might if contemplating a fat figure on the latest bank statement.

And therein lies his real problem, though crops and vines and flocks blind him to it. The problem of storing all this abundance sends him looking for a wise consultant. That may be smart, but his choice of adviser isn't. The only person he seems to consult is himself. And this self has a very narrow perspective, bounded on every side by prospects of the good life—for himself. Forget family—and in a rural Palestinian family relatives were sure to include at least one impoverished cousin or struggling widow or orphaned youngster, never mind aging parents or wife and children. And a destitute neighbor or perhaps the leper colony over the hill where Aunt

Martha disappeared years ago? Not even a blip in the ledger. The farmer is clearly the sole beneficiary of his own insurance plan. So, reasonably, when he needs to know what to do, he asks himself.

And, as the psalmist says, "In his riches, man cannot discern" (Ps 49:21). His self makes big plans. Barns built for last year's crops too small? Go to town and hire cheap day laborers to tear them all down and build bigger ones. Much bigger! The fact that the existing barns seem to be empty enough of last year's harvest to tear down doesn't seem to give him a minute's pause. Last year is dead and gone. All his blinkered self can see is that bright future. Rose-colored glasses might not have been invented yet, but he certainly has a pair of first-century equivalents!

He might have made better plans if he had consulted a wiser adviser. The Adviser he didn't consult at all was forced to stay silent. God is too courteous to offer unwanted counsel. But the divine arbiter is finally forced to step in at the end and douse the farmer's celebration with a large bucket of cold reality. The time has come, God says, for a harvest the barn builder has not planned on.

Jesus offers the parable as a cautionary tale to all of us would-be barn builders. Rather than filling all those barns on earth to the roof, he says, you might want to pay some attention instead to filling the barns awaiting you in heaven. And you can do that only by filling on this earth the barns of those without the means to fill their own. Indeed, they actually have no need of barns, because it is all they can do to put food on the table for the next meal, to provide their family a roof that doesn't leak and walls made of something stronger than cardboard. Many can't do even that. And then there are those others whose barns stand empty not of grain, wine, and oil but of simple human kindness, a bit of attention in their loneliness, a word of hope in their discouragement, some connection that will redeem them from their soul-destroying isolation. It does take time, effort, and a few of the goods out of your own barns, it's true. But you might want to do it anyway. Because that final harvest, the one the barn builder in the parable did not expect, will come.

At the Pharisee's Dinner Party
Luke 7:36-50

This little masterpiece offers, in quick succession, an uneasy dinner party, a dramatic interruption, a bewildering commentary, a Pharisee put in his place, a sinner forgiven.

Because stories like this have become so familiar from much hearing and much preaching, we may be tempted to jump too soon to the drama supplied by the sinful intruder weeping over Jesus' feet, wiping them with her hair, and anointing them with ointment from the finest of jars. Let's begin instead at the beginning. Although Jesus is best remembered for sitting at table with obvious sinners like tax collectors and prostitutes, he also accepted dinner invitations from "more respectable" people like Simon the Pharisee. As we watch host and guests reclining at table, we recognize that we are in foreign territory. It is obviously a formal dinner, but where are the table and chairs, the linen napkins and the gleaming silver, the candelabra? This is certainly not Downton Abbey. Miss Manners offers no advice about protocol for an occasion like this one.

The unfamiliar setting is not the only cause of our unease. We are a bit surprised to see a Pharisee hosting the carpenter from Galilee. We are accustomed to fireworks, not dinner table pleasantries, between the Pharisees and Jesus. Simple, friendly table chat seems unlikely.

In this unaccustomed situation, what should we expect?

Certainly not what happens. In comes a gate-crasher, and not just any gate-crasher. She is a woman, one recognized as a sinner by the diners. The customary assumption is that she is a prostitute. Perhaps she is. However, Luke does not say. Perhaps she tells fortunes, perhaps she peddles suspicious potions, or perhaps she has had multiple husbands and now lives with a man to whom she is not married, like the Samaritan woman at the well (John 4:17-19). Whatever her sin, it has been flagrant enough to make her persona non grata at the Pharisee's table.

Even before the nard and the hair-as-towel, the woman startles us by her intrusion. She must know the rules convention lays out for her: She should not enter someone else's house uninvited when he has guests at table, never mind that the outraged host is a prominent Pharisee, upholder of rigid religious observance, and the guests are equally respectable Pharisees and an itinerant rabbi who is fast becoming a celebrity. She should not go anywhere near Jesus, a man, a holy man by all accounts, much less touch him or bathe his feet with her tears and wipe them with her hair. Her hair? Unveiled in the presence of these eminent men? Worse yet, she goes so far as to kiss his bare feet—he would have left his sandals at the door—and pour precious ointment all over them from an alabaster jar. Alabaster? Nard *and* alabaster? Are they the profit of her sin? One can feel the shock and indignation rising in the room.

Simon thinks dark thoughts, not about the woman, who has earned them, but about Jesus, who has done nothing but fail to push her away. If the Pharisee had thought it through, he might have realized that a man who lays his hands on lepers is hardly going to chase off a weeping woman who lays hands on his feet, however inappropriately. Lepers one could perhaps excuse, since he heals them, though they are legally off limits under the code of purity laws so insistently defended by the Pharisees. But a public sinner, a woman at that, a woman embarrassing all of them with her dramatic extravagance? Could one imagine Elijah or Jeremiah or one of the other great prophets allowing such liberties from a female in every way unclean? Simon thinks not. He and his guests begin to wonder if Jesus is a prophet at all.

They have apparently forgotten how awkward the prophets could be about respecting empty proprieties. However, Jesus, quite mildly, simply tells them a story about two debtors. One owes a paltry sum, the other a fortune to the same creditor. The creditor forgives both debts. In the manner of a rabbi, Jesus asks a simple question: "Which of the debtors would love the creditor more?" "Love" seems an odd word to use about any relationship between debtors and creditors. Simon should perhaps have been warned that something unexpected was afoot. However, he simply follows the logic of the story and falls into the trap so neatly set for him: "The one, I suppose, with the larger debt."

Now Jesus, in the manner of Elijah or Ezekiel, pounces. Right you are, he says to Simon. Then, leaving story for reality, he turns convention upside down by simply comparing the woman's behavior with Simon's, to Simon's discredit. Simon has committed no major sins, of course, merely breaches in the code of etiquette. When Jesus came in, dusty from the road, Simon did not offer him the customary water jug, basin, and towel with which to wash his feet. He did not offer him the kiss expected between host and guest, something like a welcoming handshake in our day. He did not pour the customary olive oil over Jesus' head to refresh him from the ravages of the Palestinian sun. But the woman, the sinner, has made up for Simon's discourtesy by doing all of those things, albeit with a bit more flair. And she has clearly not acted out of mere custom. After all, she is not the hostess but a gate-crasher. Which one, Jesus might have asked, has respected the code of etiquette for welcoming a guest?

To everyone's surprise, Jesus does far more than that. With breathtaking audacity, he makes it clear that the woman so readily condemned by his host and fellow diners is in fact no longer a sinner. Her sins have been forgiven. We sometimes misread the story and conclude she has been pardoned because of her dramatic foot washing, but that does not seem to be what Jesus actually says. Since she interrupted the dinner party, the woman has made no confession and asked no forgiveness. Clearly Jesus knows her better than Simon and the others. The story of debtors and creditor suggests that he knows she was indeed a sinner but has come into the house a woman already pardoned. She has asked for nothing at all. Rather, she has been expressing deep gratitude for the forgiveness of what must have been great sins. One can imagine that Jesus understands because he was the one who forgave her before she ever showed up in Simon's dining room.

Simon, on the other hand, is skewered by his own discourtesies. They were not as petty as they sound to us, living as we do in a world where both manners and hospitality are far less valued than they were in Jesus' day. Simon's neglect of his guest was a violation of the code of hospitality, held sacred in the Middle East from ancient times. It was, in fact, a not-so-veiled insult. "The one to whom little is forgiven, loves little," Jesus says. You, Simon, are he. We cannot help wondering whether the reason little has been forgiven is that Simon has asked no forgiveness, perhaps secure in his conviction of his own righteousness despite his offensive behavior toward his guest. Yet when both the sinful woman and the Pharisee are weighed in the scales of God's peculiar sense of righteousness, it is, quite unexpectedly, the Pharisee who is found wanting.

With all the courtesy Simon is lacking, Jesus, the woman's true host at this gathering, turns and reassures her of her real standing: "Your sins are forgiven." Go on home, he might have said. *You* have nothing to be ashamed of.

At the end of the day, the sinner is vindicated, the self-righteous reproved, and Jesus once more revealed as "the wisdom of God" (1 Cor 1:24). Compassionate, fearless, clever, he makes an appealing hero for the tale.

That does not excuse him from getting a bit too close to home. My home. The woman's demonstrative extravagance has always made me uneasy. Such flamboyance does not appeal to me, or so I say to excuse my discomfort with a woman of whom Jesus so clearly approves. Simon is somehow a less alien figure. I know I have been forgiven much. I claim to love the Pardoner. But I'm very much afraid that Simon's pinch-penny welcome is far more like the kind of greeting I give Jesus when he chooses to come to dinner at my house (cf. Rev 3:20).

Martha and Mary: Disciples of the Lord
Luke 10:38-42; John 11:17-27

Let's dismantle the story of hyperactive Martha trying to drag Jesus into a triangulation to convey her displeasure with her lazy, "contemplative" sister. While we're about it, let's also jettison the guilt felt by countless busy religious people who cast a sideways glance, not always envious, at the "contemplatives" bathed in candlelight and incense, basking in the assurance that they have chosen the "one thing necessary," or "the better part," depending on the translation.

For one thing, the Gospels offer us no reason to discount Martha. She might not have been busy about "the one thing necessary," but she *was* busy about the holy work of hospitality. Think about the story of Jesus' raising Peter's mother-in-law out of her sickbed (Mark 1:29-31). Her first act wasn't to take a shower or report to her friends. It was to fix her visitors a meal. Sickness had deprived her of this privileged responsibility, deeply cherished in Middle Eastern culture, including the biblical world. Jesus' healing allowed her to take it up again. So Martha is carrying on a tradition highly revered. Moreover, John 11:5 tells us that Jesus loved both Martha and Mary, along with their brother Lazarus, who does not feature in the Lucan story.

Mary, on the other hand, is doing something odd in Luke 10. Even though Jesus is a guest at Martha's invitation, Mary neglects the duties that the sacred custom of hospitality would normally impose on her as a member of the family, so she's flying in the teeth of convention. And in more ways than one! Luke tells us, "she sat beside the Lord at his feet," normally the posture of a disciple. In her time and place, a woman would not ordinarily presume to cast herself in that role.

Jesus doesn't defend Mary on the grounds of her nonconformity. He seems instead to commend her because she has chosen to "[listen] to him speak" (Luke 10:39). Listening does not necessarily make her a contemplative. It does make her exactly what would have appalled her contemporaries: a disciple.

I would like to suggest that we might read "the better part" or "the one thing necessary" not so much as *what* Mary is doing—listening—praiseworthy as that is. I would suggest that the one thing necessary is the choice of *where* she is. Martha is presumably fussing over food in the other room, if the house has one, or at least in another part of the room where things like vegetables and platters and bread take up all her attention. Mary has chosen instead to be with Jesus. Listening, prayer, and discipleship all begin with the decision to be right where Mary is.

Where does that leave Martha? Should she hang up her apron and sit down at Jesus' feet also? If she does, he and his disciples will get no dinner—and this is the Teacher who lists feeding the hungry as one of the criteria for joining the sheep rather than the goats in the story of the last judgment (Matt 25:31-46)! No, there is no need to close the soup kitchen or the family dining room so everyone can go to church for an hour or two or three. No need even to listen to taped Bible readings while chopping the carrots, though some might find that helpful. What Jesus calls for is for Martha and her heirs to be with him in the midst of potato peelings and frying pans. Martha wasn't. If she had been with him at heart, she would never have sniped at her sister for following her particular call and making extra work for Martha. Her concern was obviously with herself—not a concern Jesus recommended among the great commandments (cf. Matt 22:35-40).

Martha was definitely with him in mind and heart the next time he visited though, or at least the next time recorded in the Gospel (John 11:17-27). When her brother Lazarus fell sick and Jesus failed to arrive on time to save him, Martha fussed at him a bit: "Lord, if you had been here, my brother would not have died." But even with sealed tomb visible in the background somewhere, Martha was able to say, "[But] even now I know that whatever you ask of God, God will give you." Jesus tested the boundaries of her belief a little: "Your brother will rise." And Martha replied by affirming her faith in the standard Pharisaic belief that the dead will rise on the last day. But then Jesus pushed past the boundaries into the impossible: "I am the resurrection and the life; whoever believes in me, even if he dies, will live, and everyone who lives and believes in me will never die. Do you believe this?" And Martha went there with him: "Yes, Lord. I have come to believe that you are the Messiah, the Son of God, the one who is coming into the world." Oh yes, Martha had by then clearly chosen the better part too. Hers is in fact a story of conversion, though no evangelist chooses to tell it. No wonder in later liturgical calendars she earned the title "Disciple of the Lord" first allotted implicitly to her sister.

At the end of Matthew's Gospel, Jesus makes the one promise that makes all our listening, prayer, and discipleship possible: "I am with you always" (Matt 28:20). That statement hides a question: "But will you be with me?" Mary's answer was yes. And so was Martha's. That is the one thing necessary.

The Woman Taken in Adultery

John 8:2-12

She has no name, this woman taken in adultery and threatened with death by stoning. We know nothing of her but her sin. She held no other interest for the scribes and Pharisees. To them, she was mere cannon fodder in an ongoing campaign to discredit Jesus. Or worse. We may wonder at the absence of her partner who, under the law, had also earned a death sentence (Deut 22:22-24). Perhaps he was a man of eminence, even a Pharisee himself? Or perhaps the men were following the custom, sadly still prevalent in some Middle Eastern cultures, of laying all the blame for family dishonor on the adulterous woman rather than the man. Whatever the reason, the scribes and Pharisees left him out of this judicial mockery, even though both man and woman had obviously been caught in the act. They may have been cunning enough to think the woman might evoke the greater compassion from Jesus. And it was for compassion versus fidelity to the law that they wished, in turn, to try him.

Discretion was certainly not part of their plan. They brought the woman into the very public eye of those gathered to hear the rabbi teaching in the temple area, where both speaker and place were apt to draw a crowd. They forced her to stand in the midst of those gathered, with no place to hide. How did she face them all? How did she face Jesus? With shame? Fear? Defiance? The evangelist does not tell us that either. Everything about her remains private, except her felonious disgrace. As for her accusers, they stood proud of their righteous commitment to the law of Moses. And perhaps proud of their skill in presenting Jesus with a case where only one option seemed open to him if he wanted to appear as a righteous man and teacher. The reader cannot help thinking that they hoped he would not take that option. He was not given to protecting his own reputation, especially at the expense of another's life, so that hope would not have been ill founded. In any case, they presented their trap, set and baited: "Teacher, this woman was caught in the very act of committing adultery. Now in the law, Moses commanded us to stone such women. So what do you say?"

He said nothing. The woman and her accusers stood suspended, awaiting his reply, but he merely bent down to write in the dust with his finger. To this day, no one knows what he wrote. Appeals have been made for biblical precedents to explain it. The editors of the Revised New American Bible cite as cross-reference a verse from the prophet Jeremiah condemning those who have forsaken the Lord, specifically in the Revised Standard Version: "Those who turn away from thee shall be written in the earth, for they have forsaken the LORD, the fountain of living water" (Jer 17:13).

Commentators and homilists sometimes make an intriguingly apt association with the story of Belshazzar's feast from the Book of Daniel (Dan 5:1-29), which the Pharisees may very well have known. Belshazzar, a Babylonian ruler in the line of Nebuchadnezzar, conqueror of Jerusalem and destroyer of its temple in 587/6 BC, gave the feast for a multitude of his courtiers. Under the influence of too much wine, he ordered the gold and silver vessels taken as booty from the Jerusalem temple to be brought in "so that the king, his nobles, his consorts, and his concubines might drink from them." Worse, "[w]hen the gold vessels taken from the temple, the house of God in Jerusalem, had been brought in, and while the king, his nobles, his consorts, and his concubines were drinking wine from them, they praised their gods of gold and silver, bronze and iron, wood and stone." Suddenly a mysterious disembodied hand appeared and wrote three words on the wall of the banquet hall: "MENE, TEKEL and PERES." The prophet Daniel, brought in to interpret them for the baffled banqueters, reported that God had not taken their sacrilege lightly. He said, "These words mean: MENE, God has numbered your kingdom and put an end to it; TEKEL, you have been weighed on the scales and found wanting; PERES, your kingdom has been divided and given to the Medes and Persians." And that night, Belshazzar was killed.

But both the Jeremiah and Daniel references, satisfying as they may be to curious readers, imply that Jesus' words in the sand, whatever they were, were meant to frighten his opponents or shame them by comparing them to the Gentile destroyer of the temple. But Jesus never sought to destroy his enemies. On the contrary, as he had taught his disciples to do, he prayed for them. And he did so even from the cross where he asked the Father to forgive them because they didn't know what they were doing (Luke 23:34). How could he, who embodied the new covenant between God and humanity, the covenant whose laws could be summed up as love of God and neighbor (Matt 22:36-40), fail to love the scribes and Pharisees? As frustrated and even angry as he sometimes seemed to be at their hypocrisy, he was nevertheless grieved by their hardness of heart (Mark 3:5). Indeed, hardness of heart might supply us with a better image than Jeremiah's threat or Belshazzar's story for understanding what Jesus was about as he stooped and wrote in that sand.

Elsewhere, Jesus had compared them to "whitewashed tombs, which appear beautiful on the outside, but inside are full of dead men's bones and every kind of filth" (Matt 23:27). If we look past the hideous contents of such tombs, in themselves insulting to law-abiding scribes and Pharisees because the bones of the dead were considered unclean under the law, we see that Jesus was comparing the Pharisees' hardened hearts to stone tombs in which they themselves lay buried. In the biblical tradition, the deadened heart encased in stone was a terrible thing, but it was not incurable. The prophet Ezekiel reported God's promise to faithless Israel: "I will give you a new heart, and a new spirit I will put within you. I will remove the heart of stone from your flesh and give you a heart of flesh" (Ezek 36:26). And Jesus was sent by the Father to keep that promise to all those hardened against God's word, ultimately by taking their place in the tomb. So he wouldn't have wanted to destroy his opponents but to break open their hardened hearts and let them out.

And so he did. He neither threatened them nor shamed them. Shame was their tool, never his. When they insisted that he answer their question, he finally straightened up and said only: "Let the one among you who is without sin be the first to throw a stone at her" (John 8:7). Then he bent down and went on writing. Apparently, his words had pierced the stone encasing those hearts with the sudden recognition that they too were sinners. In fact, they and the accused woman shared that in common. It's then that we discover they had brought the sinful woman before Jesus with stones already in hand for her execution. But instead, as if the stone walls of their own sepulchers had broken and fallen down around them, they dropped the stones at their feet and walked quietly away. And Jesus even spared them the humiliation of seeing him look them in the face as they went. He continued to focus on his writing until they were gone. Perhaps it was with this encounter in mind that Jesus would say some verses later to a different audience, "you will know the truth, and the truth will set you free" (John 8:32).

When the Pharisees had left, he stood up and did for the woman what he had done for her accusers. He offered her the truth. He asked, "Has no one condemned you?" No, no one had. So Jesus said, "Neither do I condemn you. Go, [and] from now on do not sin any more." He gave her in fact a dual truth: he acknowledged that she had sinned, a fact she had never denied, and he made it clear that her "trial" had ended with no verdict. The law that could have condemned her had instead set her free to go with nothing more than a compassionate warning not to put herself in this position again—for Jesus was and is both law and judgment made flesh. And his judgment is always truth and mercy standing hand in hand.

The Widow:
Two Small Coins, So Many Questions
Luke 21:1-4

She was a widow. And she was poor. In the Scriptures, the two are often synonymous. Widows were bereft not only of their husbands but also of their primary means of support, unless they had children or other relatives able to care for them. There were rich widows, but they seem to have been rare. Poverty was the common lot of the woman left alone. Prudence would suggest that she conserve her resources. Neighbors would praise her for watching her pennies; relatives responsible for her would thank her for providing for her own needs; wisdom and custom would commend her for her caution. Yet here she was, bringing her last small coins to the temple and casting them, unasked, among the offerings. Who would commend her for that bit of pious foolishness?

Jesus did. He saw something most bystanders would not. He saw that she saw something most bystanders would not recognize. Ordinary folk, ruled by ordinary common sense, would look at the two coins and see that they would not go far to feed and clothe her and keep a roof over her head. She looked at the coins and saw that God had given them to her to use for the divine glory or for someone else's good. Ordinary folk would look at her and see that she was in peril of perishing in her poverty. She looked at God and saw that divine providence would not abandon her. Ordinary folk would see that she had nothing. She saw that she had God. Ordinary folk would call her shortsighted. Jesus would no doubt have called her very farsighted indeed because, where others saw only the very real short-term consequences of what she had done, she saw beyond them into the reign of God.

Or so we might read her story. The Gospel, in its usual maddening way, draws us into this tiny event by baiting it with unanswered questions: Was she truly alone or did she have family? Why did she choose to give away her last two coins? Did she know where the next one would come from? And why on God's green earth did Jesus praise her? Surely he did not mean we should imitate her?

We can only wonder. Jesus left the scene without any explanation.

The Bethesda Story: The Man at the Pool

John 5:1-14

Bethesda was a popular spa in Jesus' day, but a spa with a difference. You didn't have to be rich or famous to stay there. You only had to be sick. Well, sick and desperate, maybe. People did say that when an angel stirred up the waters, the first one in would be cured. If you'd been there long enough, you might have seen it work for other people like you, sick and desperate and willing to believe anything if it would make them well. Why not? It's not like a sick man could work or a sick woman keep house for her family. Probably easier on relatives to leave you there for a while than to deal with you at home. Being on the spot at the right time was your only hope anyway. But for those who lay there, this was no vacation spa. It was a way of life.

So it was for the sick man in John's story. He had been there for thirty-eight years. Thirty-eight! Well more than half a lifetime in those days. He might have started out with options. It sounds as if he could at least make his way to the pool somehow. He just couldn't get there fast enough. Meanwhile, maybe he could get around one of the porticoes a little, visit with others like himself who had no one in particular to take care of them, tell stories of the good old days, complain about the heat.

Or maybe not. The story doesn't say how the man occupied the endless hours of those thirty-eight years. To have been there so long, he must have started out very young, as full of hope as any invalid taking the waters at a modern spa or signing up for the latest experimental treatment. But when the hours became days and the days years, hope settled down in a corner and fell asleep. You can get used to anything after a while, even to life on a mat by a pool where everyone lives for a little ripple in the water. The mat becomes home, the poolside your village, your illness a friend and companion. Ask anyone who has given up on escaping whatever sickness has moved in and set up housekeeping in the soul.

Maybe you know the feeling yourself. Lent after Lent after Lent, you say to yourself, "This year I'm gonna lick that habit. I'll quit overeating, or bickering with my family, or checking out another pile of mysteries from the library. I'll do something good for someone instead. And I'll pray more." But somehow you don't. At end of Lent, you say with a sigh, "Next year for sure!" But after years and years of being stuck in that same old place, you've really given up believing it. Sick, or addicted, or sinful, or weak, or whatever other adjective you've attached to your worst habit, you shrug your shoulders and say, "That's just who I am!" and give up any hope of change. Like that man on the mat by the pool.

Jesus came as a bit of a shock to the sick man. He does that. He didn't ask, "How are you?" He didn't murmur sympathies. He didn't offer, "Can I bring you a loaf of fresh bread or a jug of water?" He went right to the heart of the matter: "Do you want to be well?" Now that sounds like one of the world's dumbest questions at a time like that, even if Jesus is the one asking. The guy has been sitting there for thirty-eight years. How could he not want to be well? He explains patiently, "I've tried. I've tried over and over. But I don't get around very well. And I have no help. Family's too busy, no one cares anymore, my friend Joseph who used to give me a hand died last year, and he was as slow as I am anyway, and the sun is hot, makes it hard to move fast, so I'm just stuck here, year after year." A statement of fact, with a hint of a whine lurking behind the words? Certainly the best of excuses.

You may know that routine too. You do try to get up from the place where you're stuck, you really do, but you try a little less hard every year. You find excuses, good ones, flimsy ones, any ones. Mostly they come down to, "I can't. I'm too weak. And besides, I'm used to the way I am." The truth is it's easier to hang onto the mat by the pool than to keep making the effort to get up and go. Most of us have been there at some time or another. Maybe we still are. One more Lent has come and gone, one more Easter dawned among the lilies and the alleluias, but nothing has changed. We don't want to admit that the unvaried monotony of our crippling routines gives us a certain security. So we settle down under the cover of thinking we're just victims of circumstance, that nameless, faceless, unbeatable oppressor of the helpless, and we get comfortable there because we believe in our bones we're not going anywhere else.

Jesus intrudes on all that comfort. He must have recognized that down deep somewhere, in a place the sick man never visited anymore for fear of the disappointment, he really did want to get well. A small, unacknowledged glimmer of desire is enough for Jesus to work with, it seems. He tells the sick man, "Rise, take up your mat, and walk." The man could have refused, I suppose. You can turn your back even on Jesus if you really want to. But to give the sick man credit, he dropped all the nice, safe excuses and got up, picked up his mat, and walked away from pool and portico and out into the street.

The Pharisees offered him one last excuse to go back to his old ways—there are always relatives or so-called friends waiting to do that. They told him that carrying his mat on the Sabbath was against God's law. It was, of course, or at least it was against customary interpretations added to the simple commandment, "Keep holy the Sabbath." But the sick man, or rather the formerly sick man, must have wanted to laugh in their faces. "I've been lying at Bethesda for thirty-eight years. Thirty-eight years! During all that time, none of you cared what I was doing. Now, a man comes along and changes my life with a word, and all you can say is that carrying my mat is against the law? Give me a break. He told me to get up, so I got up. He told me to carry my mat, so I'm carrying it. And who do you think is behind it all if not the God you're so eager to protect from the likes of me? Forget it. I'm going to the temple to say thank you!" He may not have said all that. One didn't mess with the religious leaders of the day. But he may very well have thought it.

At any rate, he did go to the temple. Jesus found him there. And delivered the zinger: "Sin no more . . ."

What Jesus is saying to the sick man is that, no matter what he may have thought, no matter what excuses he has hidden behind for thirty-eight years, he is no victim. He is standing upright now and walking, but it's up to him to decide what direction he will take from here on out. He has options: back to the mat by the pool or forward into a new life that will take effort, work, disappointments, triumphs, time to build. Jesus has given him the power to choose, even to choose to walk away from the pool for good. But now it's up to him.

Easter is very scary. We stand outside the tomb, our tomb, and realize all too clearly that we have the power to climb back in, roll that stone over the door from inside, and hide there.

There will be days when we miss the comfort of the old ways, the security of our sinfulness, the safety of those stone walls we've wrapped around ourselves. But let's not go. Jesus is out here in the light inviting us to follow on down the road.

Today is the day the Lord has made! Let us rejoice and be glad! And walk on in his footsteps!

Judas: Mirror and Mystery

Matthew 26:14-16

Judas is a question mark: why did he do it? Matthew tells us what Judas did, but he doesn't tell us why. Down through the centuries, readers and commentators, librettists and screenwriters have filled in the blanks: he did it for the money, he did it because Jesus had failed to live up to his expectations of a political messiah, he did it because the devil made him do it, he did it . . . well, no one knows why he did it.

As we listen to the story, Judas becomes a mirror the Gospel holds up to us. In it we see the face of our own betrayals looking back at us. Piety may forbid us to see anything but horror in Judas for what he did. After all, he sold Jesus to his torturers and murderers. But honesty requires us to admit that he is not alone in having sold for small change the one thing that mattered. How many of us have sold our prayer for entertainment, our integrity for power or prestige, our life's work for an easy ride? Is selling God's gifts for a handful of trifles any less heinous, really, than selling the Savior?

Come now, you're probably saying, there's no comparison. I've made my little compromises, sure, but nobody died for it. Is that really true? Jesus, Son of God, died in a few hours on one particular afternoon, but the echoes have reverberated among believers and doubters alike ever since. We, the children of God, die no less decisively when we trade away our own God-given truth over a lifetime of little compromises. St. Basil the Great defines sin as the use of God's gifts for purposes other than those for which they were given. Most grievous, he says, is the misuse of love—our love for God, our love for those among whom we were planted in this world, our love for those to whom we can offer some service through the talents and tasks God has given us. A gifted storyteller puts the gift to use writing trash for cash. A gifted artist devotes a lifetime to producing commercials peddling luxuries rather than painting great masterpieces. A gifted singer forces a soaring voice into a style that damages it for the sake of a place in the top ten. A gifted parent sacrifices time for the family in favor of clean and lovely surroundings or a weekend in front of the TV or a fishing trip. Not major crimes, surely? Ah, but the serpent's tooth poisons by small bites. And the serpent's whisper is well disguised as "everybody does it" or "you owe it to yourself" or "come on—be practical."

After a while, maybe, we forget we have options. We may well have our little stash of silver coins hidden somewhere, rewards for our betrayals of true selves, but it's never too late to trade them in again for forgiveness, freedom, life. The loss may be painful, the prospect of change frightening, the way back long and hard. But the offer is always there.

Jesus forgave Peter, who denied him, and the other disciples who abandoned him, and even the men with hammer and nails who crucified him. Surely he was just as ready to forgive Judas. Why didn't Judas accept? Why didn't he allow the Savior to save him from his own despair? Why did he hang himself after three years in the company of God's mercy-made-flesh

(Matt 27:5)? I wonder if it was because he had so eroded his soul with a lifetime of betrayals that he could no longer see the outstretched hand. Having walled himself into the very small cell of his own self-interest and shame, perhaps he could no longer recognize that the door stood open. And who knows? Maybe, in the privacy of one of those moments of anguish and mercy that go unreported by the evangelists—who had reason to think ill of Judas anyway—God finally managed to pry open Judas's fist and fill it with something far better than thirty pieces of silver. I hope so. But what went on for Judas in his darkness remains as much a question as his motives.

If Judas is question, puzzle, thorn in the flesh of the Christian mind, he is also, like all of us, mystery. How many of us can really fathom in ourselves the depths where betrayal and grace meet? I would rather not reduce Judas to a simple explanation. I would rather allow him to remain a mirror. If I can't see into his soul, perhaps he can let me see into mine. My prayer is for the courage to look.

The Cup: James and John

Mark 10:35-45

They seem young, James and John. All that dashing grandiosity! Earlier Jesus nicknamed them the "Sons of Thunder" (Mark 3:17). Perhaps they had earned it by wanting to call down fire from heaven on the Samaritan village that refused entry to Jesus' band (Luke 9:51-56). Jesus stopped their brewing thunderstorm in mid-rumble, amused perhaps by their youthful eagerness to imitate the prophet Elijah calling down lightning on soldiers sent to arrest him (2 Kgs 1:10, 12).

The imagery would have been clearer to them than it is to us. "Cup" was a frequent biblical metaphor for "destiny." Among the prophets, the cup was usually the fate that awaited Jerusalem: the "cup of wrath," "cup of staggering," "cup of drugged wine" all earned by the people's infidelity (e.g., Isa 51:17; Ezek 23:32-33). Who would step up for those drinks?

Jesus will. In Gethsemane, confronted with a threatening tomorrow, he agonizes, "Take this cup away from me, but not what I will but what you will" (Mark 14:36). He knows what that cup will hold: the wine pressed from the wild grapes yielded by rebellious Israel. Treasured as God's vine, it detached itself from the trellis of the Torah and wandered off into the cold shade cast by sin and death. Grapes deprived of sunlight harden and yield thin, sour wine (cf. Isa 5:1-4). Israel, indeed all of humanity, deserves the cup, but Jesus takes it up in our stead. John, with his eye for symbol, bypasses the agony in the garden. Rather, he reports Jesus saying on the cross, "I thirst" (John 19:28). The soldiers offer him not the drugged wine of Mark's Gospel but the common wine they had on hand (John 19:29; cf. Mark 15:23). Jesus swallows it, then says, "It is finished." And so it is. The "cup" has been drunk down.

Young James and John could not have known these details, but Jesus warns them: he has come not to be served festal wine but to provide it, offering his life as a ransom for many (cf. Mark 10:25). But the two boys have already cast aside home, family, and a profitable fishing business to follow him. Why stop now?

They don't. They take the cup. James will eventually die a martyr. John will accept exile into old age. Jesus might say they took the plunge—the meaning of the Greek root for "baptism"—and followed him through the valley of death into the glory they so longed for, bringing with them the countless believers for whom they poured out their own lives in service of Jesus' word and work.

The story goes on. We have also taken the plunge in baptism and gathered at the Eucharistic table to accept the cup. James and John remind us those choices are no mere ritual but a way of life—and even death.

Sarah

A Story (Genesis 12–23)

Sarah awakened swiftly, as desert-dwellers must, to a sense of something wrong. She could not tell what it was. Outside the tent, the animals stirred in rustling restlessness, but they raised no alarm. Inside, the oldest of the serving women snored lightly as she usually did until her younger companion tired of her and poked her to turn over. And none too gently, either, the old woman used to complain, when the younger slave had been Hagar. "Hagar! Minx!" thought Sarah sleepily, remembering. The venom that still rose at the thought of Hagar startled Sarah more widely awake. Hagar was long gone, she reassured herself at once. She was dead in the desert, she and the boy.

The boy. Her thoughts flew swiftly, as they always did, to her own Isaac. Isaac, laughter born of tears, fruit born of barrenness, hope born of despair. Isaac, her only child, her son. The thought of him stirred a sudden fear. She rose quickly—and then remembered, with bitter disappointment, that he no longer slept in his accustomed place. From birth, he had been sheltered in a little alcove within carpeted tent walls, to keep out the night air, between her own bed and the place where the slave women slept. As the boy grew out of infancy, Abraham protested against such coddling, but he had learned that one does not argue with a lioness who has only one cub, and that one born out of season. He understood, and held his tongue.

Abraham. She was distracted by the question that had plagued her since the evening before. What had happened to him? He had always been a vigorous man, strong beyond his years, unquestioned leader, father, ruler to his swarming household. But last night every one of his years had appeared all at once etched up on his face, and his years were many. She had asked him the reason of course, but he would not say. A man of many silences, her husband. She found them irritating. She liked to know what was going on in every corner of their busy world, especially in the corner occupied by her immediate family. It must have been the Voice, she thought suddenly. Yes, that must be it. Abraham had been as he always was until he went out to pray in the first shadows of the swift desert dusk, as he did every evening. When he had returned to the camp, he had walked as if the whole weight of a long life had fallen full upon him. She had never before thought him an old man. The Voice must have done that.

Abraham had gone in to see Isaac then. There had been some stir among the serving men and beasts, some preparations being made.

Sarah was once more afraid. If anything happened to her son . . . impossible. The Voice posed no threat to the boy. Indeed, the child had been born to redeem some pledge the Voice had made to Abraham years before. It had seemed such a wild promise then: descendants as countless as the stars, heirs to all of Canaan, a blessing to the whole earth. Sarah had never put much faith in all that extravagance. She had known by then anyway that she was far too old to give her husband children. But Abraham had never doubted.

He was a good man, and she could not bear to see him disappointed. That was why she had given him the slave girl, Hagar, to bear him the son he longed for. When Hagar had given birth to Ishmael, the promise seemed to have been fulfilled. For all his father's delight, he might as well have been a skyful of stars. But then those odd strangers had come. And the following year, her son had been born, her Isaac, and with him this fierce unreasoning desire to keep him safe.

That was what had driven her to demand that Abraham send Hagar away, Hagar and her son, into the desert to die. He had not wanted to do it, of course, but she would not let her Isaac grow up to face an older rival. Hagar and her boy were dead, she was sure of it. The danger had died with them. Nothing could happen to her son now, nothing. But Sarah was uneasy. She did not entirely trust the Voice.

She should not, she knew, visit the tent to which her son had been moved, at his father's insistence, now that he had come of age. His mother was proud, of course, but she could not so quickly give up the habit of hovering over her nestling, even though he had grown wings. Not such strong wings yet. His voice still quavered on the threshold between childhood and manhood. She could at least walk over to see that his little household slept peacefully in the new tent. There were guards, of course, but guards were not a mother. She would not go in. She would not even go too close. She would simply go to the edge of the women's portion of the camp and look across. No harm in that, surely?

As she slipped from her own tent, she was startled to find her husband also out of doors. Nearby, a slave was loading wood on one of the pack animals. Abraham did not see her. He stood at the top of a small rise not far from the tents. She could see him in profile, outlined in black against the dark of an early morning sky as yet untouched by any hint of dawn. His face was turned toward the heavens. His lips were moving, but he seemed not to be praying. He was pointing a moving finger skyward at nothing unusual that she could see.

Suddenly, she understood. Abraham was counting stars.

Salt Tears

A Prose Poem (Genesis 19:1-29)

She stood and watched the city burn, and wept salt tears. Her maid cried out, "Come, mistress, come. The beasts are loaded, and the drivers curse. No use to look. Your house is gone. I saw it fall. We saved what bits we could. The city will be rubble soon. The household waits. Come, mistress, come."

"I come, I come," she said—but did not come. She stood and watched the city burn, and wept salt tears.

Her daughters begged, "Come, Mother, come. The air grows hot, the sky rains death, and we are desolate. No use to look. Our men have mocked their way to hell, our children are but dreams and dust. The city will be ashes soon, a memory on the wind. We need you now. Come, Mother, come."

"I come, I come," she said—but did not come. She stood and watched the city burn, and wept salt tears.

Her mother called, "Come, foolish girl. Forget your scented afternoons, your silken sleep. Past pleasures reek of hot, charred air. Old friendships are but embers now, the streets a charnel house. What's past is past. Look back no more. Your duty lies ahead. Come, come along."

"I come, I come," she said—but did not come. She stood and watched the city burn, and wept salt tears.

At last her husband came, summoned from the stir of flock and herd. "Come, woman, come. Look to the living, not the dead. The city's gone. Another lies before us. What we built once, we will rebuild again. Beloved, come."

Lot came too late. She could no longer hear. She stood where she will always stand, forever looking back to watch the city burn, a pillar of salt tears.

✝

*Palace Slave**

A Memoir (Matthew 14:3-12; Mark 6:17-29)

We palace slaves, we knew who was strongest in Herod's royal household. And it was not the king.

But one of the king's birthdays stands out in my long memory of life here in his palace.

The celebration ended with the usual banquet-cum-brawl. (You will have to forgive me my harsh judgments. I am Greek, like many of the slaves in this household. A man of education. A man of culture. For all the good it has done me.) The evening guttered in its cups, the failing torches veiled the room in clouds of smoke, but Herod was too drunk to realize that his guests, not all as drunk as he was, wanted their escape. He called for dancers.

One dancer appeared. Herodias's daughter. As the flutes began to play, she closed her eyes, rapt in the music. Her mother had tried to teach her sensuality and sinuousness, but those fell from her shoulders like discarded drapery. What she saw behind her closed eyelids, what she heard, was a different kind of song. One of the flute players caught her mood and turned it into music. The melody soared beyond the room, unveiling now a waterfall, then a hidden bed of violets, now cedars of Lebanon, then a stream leaping down wild hillsides. I recognized him then. He was a Lebanese lad who had never adjusted to his slavery. He played what he was ordered to play, but he wove into the music all the passion of a homesick heart for a land he will never see again. He and the girl understood one another, it seemed. She danced beauty, she danced loneliness, she danced flashes of water, threads of sunlit air, the music of water falling over rock. She and the boy together painted worlds no one who saw or heard them could ever forget. Even Herod was transfixed.

When the music at last fell away, and she was still, head bowed beneath the swirling veils of smoke, the king pounded on the table and demanded hoarsely, "Bring her here."

"Tell me, child," he said when she stood before him, eyes cast down, trembling slightly, "what reward I can give you. A quarter of my kingdom, by God. No, a half!"

She said nothing. She fled across the room to the woman standing in the doorway watching. Herodias. King and queen, they stared at one another across the floor. She had trapped him. Again. His anger flared but died, quenched by her cold, hard stare. We all knew who would win. We had always known. A small cat's smile played across her painted lips. Rumor whispered that it was she who had ended her marriage to the king's brother for a husband with better prospects, that it was she who had insinuated into the king's mind a growing urgency to marry her, she who had signed the wedding contract first.

Her daughter whispered into her ear. The cat smile widened. She murmured her instructions and sent the girl back across the room to deliver them. White with shock, the girl did as she was told. One did not disobey the queen.

"His head?" the king shouted, stunned. "His head on a platter? Why not gold from Solomon's mines, diamonds from the south, rubies . . . His head?"

It was not the girl he was asking but the woman in the doorway. Her smile never faltered. She nodded once. It had the feel of a sword falling.

Unbelieving Greek I may be, but by God, I would not want to see a holy man, a prophet, beheaded and displayed like that. He had dared to haul her sins out of the dark in which she concealed them, cloaked in rumor. Herodias always went half veiled in dusky shadows that masked her age and her debauchery alike. He had dared to expose her to the light. Only the glittering hardness of her eyes revealed her truth: it was power she craved, not fleshly satieties. And John had challenged that craving, claiming she was subject to the law, and condemned by it. She had let him languish in prison for a while, protected by her husband's fearful curiosity. She could afford to wait. She knew this evening must come.

When the grim platter arrived, she made the girl carry it across the room. Gone was the music, gone the waterfalls and the violets, gone the sunlight that had shone through her. Although there was not much blood, she appeared to be veiled in gore, her eyes fixed on the prophet's unclosed and unseeing eyes, her dancing feet unsteady now. One of the other slaves took the platter from her as she was about to drop it at the king's feet.

The king and queen kept their eyes fixed on one another over the hideous remains. His were the first to fall, as we could have predicted.

Neither of them noticed when the girl fled. She was never seen in public again. Herod lost interest. Her mother forgot her.

We see to it that she is well looked after. The Lebanese boy plays for her when he can slip away. We consider it our privilege to care for her. We had learned that we were wrong when we thought we knew who was the strongest in this palace. It is not Herodias after all.

Instead, it gives us hope amid the terrible wickedness of this place to know there is a light that the surrounding darkness will never quite extinguish. She is not the source of the light, I think, but she is its bearer. Who kindled that light in her, I do not know. Certainly not her mother. She is all darkness, that one. Perhaps it was the holy man. One of the guards says she carried stolen bread to him sometimes in his prison. I suppose she could have. She is kind in her quiet way, and no one paid her any heed. And I have heard it said that he claimed not to be the light but only to testify to the one who was. It doesn't matter. Whatever the light's source, I know that it is real. I saw that dance.

* The unnamed dancer of this Gospel is an elusive figure. Later tradition identifies her as Herodias's daughter Salome. The Gospels do not tell us what happened to her after that dreadful evening. Later sources supply conflicting accounts.

The Rich Young Man

A Memoir (Mark 10:17-31; Matthew 19:16-30; cf. Luke 18:18-30)

You've heard my story, of course. Everyone has by now. Everyone interested in the Master, anyway. How he looked at me with love, as they put it, and invited me to take that one last step, the one I had asked him to show me. "Sell all you have," he said, this man who had left behind far more than any of us understood then. "Give the proceeds to the poor, then come, follow me." I wanted to, you understand. I wanted to with every fiber of my being. Except one: I had responsibilities, important ones. I was the eldest, you see, and it was up to me to care for the family's patrimony and all who depended on it. My father had left prosperous lands, vineyards, olive groves. I had a mother, three younger brothers, and four sisters who would need me to arrange marriages, to say nothing of widowed cousins, old servants and tenants to support. My brothers were too young to take charge. And, I admit it to my shame, I was accustomed to the comforts wealth afforded. The Master and his followers were always on the road, homeless and impoverished, dependent on whatever others offered. Most nights, the stars were their tent and a cloak their blanket. I couldn't live like that I thought. I just couldn't. So I turned my back on him sadly.

He was also sad, they say. It's true, though I didn't look back to see his face. I didn't have to. I felt the weight of his look of regret on my shoulders long after he had turned back to his disciples. I felt it long after I had returned home to my family, my fields, my vineyards, my olive groves. Well, if you had ever seen him look at you like that, with so much love, so much disappointment—and such forgiveness—you would understand how I felt. It wasn't losing what I had imagined was eternal life that weighed upon me. It was losing him.

Peter was the one who came after me, later. Peter, with his big mouth and his big heart. They had not forgotten me, he said. At the time, they had been shocked and baffled that one so clearly chosen could turn his back like that. But now they understood, he said. At the end, when it mattered, they had also turned their backs and fled. Even Peter. The shame of it was still etched in deep lines on his face. But he had come back for them, the Master, Peter said. As he had promised. So they began to wonder if I had ever changed my mind as they had and if I would like to come back and join them now.

Odd, it didn't seem so impossible then to think of turning my responsibilities over to my brothers, who had the same wise uncles to watch over them as I had. I didn't even find it difficult, really, to turn my back on family, fields, vineyards, olive groves and face whatever life with the other disciples would mean. The truth is that nothing could ever again be as hard as turning my back on him.

I stayed with Peter, learned from him, tried to help him as I could. Traveled with him, too. That's how I come to be here in Rome now.

They came for Peter yesterday, the soldiers. You probably know what they did to him, how he died. They will likely come for the rest of us today. So I wanted to set the story straight before I go. In case you wondered. The important thing for you to know is that he never did give up on me, the Master, and he never stopped looking on me with love. He never does. So, in answer to your question, yes, I did come back.

One can. Always.

St. Lawrence of Rome*

A Memoir

"I'm well done on this side. Turn me over."

They laugh now at a joke I never made.

Well, let them, if it spares them the horror of the fire. The real fire, I mean, not the wood-fueled flame that reddens iron and blackens flesh. The real burning.

I recognized it first in the eyes of the prefect who condemned me. Not the fire itself, but the ash. A dead man looked at me out of those eyes. Relentless greed for wealth and power had burned all else out of him long before. He had those in abundance now, the gold and the power. And having them, had nothing.

He saw me as no more than a key to the fabled treasure chests of the Church of Rome. The cold, hard glint of gold lit up his eyes as he demanded access. My Lord had once pleaded with just such a one—though one perhaps not as far gone as this man was. My Christ had begged the rich young man to trade false gold for true, so I brought before the prefect what I knew to be the Church's true treasure. When he saw the ragged little crowd—men, women, and children to whom as deacon I had sometimes managed to give bread or cast-off cloaks to shield them a little from the icy teeth of a hungry winter—he was baffled and enraged. Where were the golden chalices, he asked? Where the silver plates? He should perhaps have remembered Belshazzar's feast, I thought, where an unbelieving king had drunk from vessels stolen from God's temple and died of it, but the prefect knew no more of Belshazzar than of the Christ hidden behind these pinched faces and hunched shoulders. These *were* the Church's wealth, I explained, but he saw in them nothing but street mud to be shaken from his elegantly sandaled feet.

Pity, I thought, as I caught sight among them of the old Greek slave cast out into the streets by a dead Roman's widow. I had come to know him as a man of culture, learning, and an all-seeing wisdom born of suffering accepted. Behind him stood a young woman, eager eyes darting everywhere from a face too soon old. Two of the aging women for whom she cooked, washed, and scavenged stood beside her. One of them held tightly to the hand of a boy she tried to hide in her skirts. That wily urchin with the pickpocket fingers and the makings of a saint peeped out in awe at the granite-faced Roman. I feared suddenly what my silly pride in my little Gospel lesson—half a joke in itself, I suppose—might cost if the prefect chose to vent his frustration on them. There were soldiers enough around the room, armed and bored with too much talk and too little action, ready to slaughter them where they stood.

But the prefect had other prey in mind. He dismissed the little band of beggars with a wave of the hand, and I was left standing alone before him.

His greed for gold had been thwarted, but his hunger for power had not. He ordered me to be roasted on the gridiron—funeral baked meats that required no silver plates or golden goblets. He had his own brand of humor.

The coarsest of the soldiers took me away to a cold, dank courtyard where the fire already burned. They were not gentle. They handed me over to a filthy band of ruffians who bound me to the gridiron, licking their lips as they anticipated the screams and pleas for mercy they were used to. For it was obvious that they had done this before, and done it often. The flames on which they laid me were hot enough, but the real fire burned behind their eyes.

As I looked into their faces, I understood for the first time what my Lord's deepest suffering had been. Not the thorns or the nails but the sight of human beings-turned-torturers and mocking bystanders who banqueted on other people's pain. These men had left pity and remorse behind them long ago, burned to smoke on other gridirons, I thought. When they took hold of me, there was nothing left but glee for their grisly work.

I wondered suddenly if, however briefly, my Lord had hated his destroyers. I wondered if he had thought of summoning his Father's legions of angels to obliterate them. I wondered if that had been his last temptation.

What I saw in my own destroyers was hollow shells. They had been human beings just like me once, made in God's own image as I was. But for reasons I could not know, they had sold everything that matters for so many pleasures that fed no one but themselves—so many rolls of dice weighted against them in games no one could win, so many coins that were only hollow counterfeit. Finally, in the end, there was nothing human left. They had sacrificed it all, bit by bit, on the altars of some voracious deity, a grotesque god at whose feet his own worshipers died, a god whose very existence is parody and mockery of the God I serve. And he does exist, make no mistake about that. He exists, that pseudo-god, and he has a name, but I will not dignify him by speaking it. From death in his fires there is no resurrection. I saw then that hell is not punishment but choice.

My Lord had seen the same as I, but he had known who the true Destroyer was, and who the destroyed. And he had summoned nothing down from heaven but forgiveness. So had he refused that last temptation, and so had he died. I begged the grace to do the same.

And I shivered even as they stoked the flames higher. I could so easily have been one of them, had my Lord not found me long ago. But what about them? Had he not found them? Had he offered them other choices? Could they . . . but no, down that road lay the darkness. Suddenly afraid, I turned and threw myself into the hands of mercy instead.

I might make jokes now about the gridiron and the flames. They were mere passing moments, after all, hardly worth remembering. But I could never joke about what I saw in the faces there. Never.

Let me tell you something. Merrier martyrs than I have hurled cheerful jokes into the teeth of death. But the martyrs' final purification is not laughter. The time for mirth and shouts of joy and dancing in the street, that comes later. The martyrs' final purification is tears as we tumble headlong into heaven through the immeasurable grief of God, weeping not for us but for our murderers, cherished and lost.

* Very little is actually known about St. Lawrence, except that he was ordained a deacon by Pope Sixtus II, whom he may have followed from his native Spain to Rome. The late medieval "The Golden Legend," stories of saints compiled by Jacobus of Voragine, ascribes Lawrence's death to the Emperor Decius. However, St. Lawrence seems most likely to have been martyred shortly after his patron, in the persecution of the Emperor Valerian, around AD 258. Scholars have cast doubt on the gridiron. A contemporary edict prescribed a quick death by beheading for clergy. Lawrence entered early into legend, especially for the episode of the poor, but "The Golden Legend" popularized an existing account of his death by roasting. Voragine attributed the famous "joke" not to the saint but to the emperor.

Prayers and Psalms

Hail, Holy Queen (Salve Regina)

Hail, holy Queen, Mother of Mercy,
our life, our sweetness and our hope.
To thee do we cry, poor banished children of Eve;
to thee do we send up our sighs,
mourning and weeping in this valley of tears.
Turn then, most gracious advocate,
thine eyes of mercy toward us;
and after this our exile,
show unto us the blessed fruit of thy womb, Jesus.
O clement, O loving, O sweet Virgin Mary.
V. Pray for us, O holy Mother of God,
R. That we may be made worthy of the promises of Christ.

This prayer comes to us from medieval Europe, which was peppered with queens. Today, queens have lost most of their glamour and authority, but they still crowd our memory in splendid dress and robed with power: Elizabeth I of England, Maria Theresa of Austria, Catherine the Great of Russia.

Mary, the Mother of Jesus, hardly seems to fit among them. The Gospel of Luke suggests she was a village girl, betrothed to a working man, a carpenter. She bore her Child among beasts of burden and laid him in their manger, on a bed of straw. She fled with him into exile in enemy territory, Egypt, until it was safe for the family to go home to Nazareth. She stood beside him as he died the hideous death of a criminal. Hardly a tale of majesty!

Yet the angel Gabriel hints at queenship in promising Mary's Son an everlasting throne (see Luke 1:26-38). Similarly, Isaiah prophesied that a child would one day rule as king from David's throne (Isa 9:1-6). These passages, which are assigned to the feast of the Queenship of Mary, presume an old tradition: a king's mother holds the title of queen.

Mary likely wore homespun, but the Church has long seen her in the garb of the woman of Revelation, clothed with the sun, a crown of twelve stars on her head (Rev 12). Mary's royal robe is woven not of planetary matter but of the fire of the sun. Fire is a favorite biblical image for God. At the Transfiguration, Jesus' face shines like the sun, and his clothing is like white light. Like all Christians, Mary is clothed in Christ, the risen Sun of Justice. That is her "cloth of gold," the sign and source of her majesty.

Mary's glory reflects Christ's. He is the son of her flesh, and she is his image in spirit. We see that most clearly in her, "May it be done to me according to your word" (Luke 1:38), mirrored in his, "Not my will but yours be done" (Luke 22:42). Christ's obedience is, paradoxically, the source of his power over sin and death. Mary's obedience is an echo of his: she reigns in the Reign of God by obeying God's will. The "Hail Holy Queen" hints at the purpose of her power: she is the mother of mercy. Through her mercy, she shows us Christ, the mercy of God.

In Paradisum

May the angels lead you into paradise;
may the martyrs come to welcome you
and take you to the holy city,
the new and eternal Jerusalem.
May choirs of angels welcome you
and lead you to the bosom of Abraham;
and where Lazarus is poor no longer
may you find eternal rest.

—*Order of Christian Funerals*

We accompany our dead. We pray with them on their deathbed. We care reverently for their mortal remains. We prepare them carefully for their final rest. We gather to receive them into the assembly that was theirs, to mark with prayer their last tangible moments among us, and to escort them to the place where we must leave them, so reluctantly, to the care of other hands than ours.

As we walk with them toward burial, we begin to relinquish them to those who can accompany them beyond the borders of their new homeland. We are offered the opportunity to sing *In paradisum* ("May the angels lead . . ."), calling upon the angels, denizens of paradise, and martyrs, citizens of the new Jerusalem (cf. Rev 21), to take them from us and lead them the rest of the way, to make sure they arrive safely. As we sing, we are invited to see them upright and walking, no longer carried, toward wonder. We may add the *Chorus angelorum* ("May the choirs of angels . . .") to seek a welcome for them from the angels and from Lazarus, the poor beggar ignored by his rich neighbor but rewarded by God with eternal rest in the bosom of Abraham (Luke 16:19-31). Perhaps Lazarus was chosen because, in the story, he too suffered, died, and was carried to paradise by angels. He would know how to receive with understanding those who have just made that unfamiliar crossing.

It matters to us not simply to abandon our dead at the edge of the unseen. How much it matters becomes apparent when circumstances prevent the rites of death and burial. It matters too that we not be abandoned, we who have had to watch our departed go from us into the company of strangers. In praying these texts, we ourselves are accompanied and comforted by the cloud of Christian mourners who have prayed the *In paradisum* since at least the ninth century. (The *Chorus angelorum* was added somewhat later.)

Even after the funeral rites are long behind us, we continue to accompany our dead with prayer, especially during the month of November. Why not borrow these ancient words from the Church and make them our own as we continue to seek safety, welcome, and rest for those we have had to leave at the door of the grave?

We accompany our dead, and we call on others to accompany them.

We accompany our dead because we love them.

We accompany our dead because we believe they live.

Anima Christi

Soul of Christ, sanctify me.
Body of Christ, save me.
Blood of Christ, inebriate me.
Water from the side of Christ, wash me.
Passion of Christ, strengthen me.
O good Jesus, hear me.
Within your wounds hide me.
Do not let me to be separated from you.
From the malicious enemy defend me.
In the hour of my death call me
and bid me come to you,
that with your saints I may praise you
for ever and ever. Amen.

Best known as a prayer after communion, the *Anima Christi* ("Soul of Christ") serves up a feast of tangible experiences to the hungry imagination. The Eucharistic imagination of the fourteenth century, when the prayer first appeared in writing, must have been starved. Worshipers were distanced from the altar by language and architecture. Communion was rare; the cup was available only to clergy. Not surprisingly, Eucharistic devotions flourished in compensation. Many of them emphasized visual access to the Eucharistic Christ through the eye of faith, but this stark list of simple petitions calls on Christ to break through the barriers of remoteness: "Do not let me to be separated from you," now or ever, is the petitioner's central cry.

What we seek is intimate, palpable contact with the Crucified One wholly present in the Eucharist: body, blood, soul, and divinity. The requests begin with abstractions—sanctify me, save me. But they move quickly to concrete actions that make the abstract real and immediate—inebriate me, wash me, strengthen me, hear me, hide me, defend me, call me.

The need is urgent: *do* something! The plea hangs there in all its burning trust, unadorned with the customary praises or even thanks.

It evokes the image of the dead but undefeated Christ hanging on the cross, his side pierced by the soldier's lance, water and blood pouring from the wound (John 19:34). Growing appreciation for the humanity of Christ, especially in his suffering and death, spawned medieval devotion not only to the pierced heart but also to all the wounds inflicted by the Passion. Texts and prayers of the time often refer to kissing, drinking from, and hiding in the wounds. It was an era less squeamish than ours about translating spiritual intimacies into physical terms! However, the imagery is heavily grounded in St. Paul's identification of the wounded Savior with the rock riven to give life-giving water to God's people in the desert (1 Cor 10:4). The notion of hiding in the "Rock of ages, cleft for me," as the old hymn proposes, gives us a vivid picture of how to enter the life "hidden with Christ in God" (Col 3:3). It thus becomes a powerful image of finding the presence, strength, protection, and refreshment we seek from the Eucharistic Christ.

It also hints at something deeper. The risen Christ appeared to his disciples with his wounds still visible. Death and resurrection had not removed them but transformed them into sources of healing, as we see in his appearance to Thomas (John 20:24-29). But they were first our wounds, the wounds of the frail mortal flesh that he assumed in all things except sin (Isa 53:4-5; Heb 4:15). Through his incarnation, passion, and death Jesus binds us to himself in one body, one new humanity (1 Cor 12; Eph 2:13-18). Thus all our wounds are still in some sense his. We find him not by hiding in his wounds to escape our own but by entering into the depths of our own wounds to find him there.

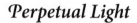

Perpetual Light

Eternal rest grant unto them, O Lord,
and let perpetual light shine upon them.

—————————

Réquiem ætérnam dona eis, Dómine,
et lux perpétua lúceat eis.

—*Order of Christian Funerals*

This little prayer has long spilled out of the funeral Mass into other occasions: visits to graves, anniversaries of deaths, even the traditional prayer after meals.

It gives me pause. Local safety codes require my monastery to keep perpetual lights shining in the hallways. The fire chief understandably does not want crews stumbling around in the smoky dark of an unfamiliar building when called to deal with a fire. So every other hall light burns 24/7. To keep expenses down, the bulbs are energy-saving white fluorescents diffused by large, round, white shades, like eyes that never close. They conceal nothing, soften nothing, miss nothing. They are not kindly lights: they deaden color, flatten textures, turn art works and people alike into ghosts of themselves. I cannot help but think of the famous line from Jean-Paul Sartre's play *No Exit:* "Hell is other people." For me that has always translated as, "Day or night, the light is always on, and eyes are always watching you."

So why would I wish perpetual light to shine on my beloved dead? And why would God wish it?

Perhaps because the Scriptures promise not white fluorescents but firelight: "The city [has] no need of sun or moon to shine on it, for the glory of God [gives] it light, and its lamp [is] the Lamb" (Rev 21:23). Not wanting Israel to sculpt idols of animal or human figures and imagine them to be divine, as their neighbors did, God seems to have favored fire as the most eloquent garb in which to appear. On Sinai, in the desert, in the Jerusalem temple, God comes clothed in the fiery cloud that came to be called God's "glory."

Shifting flames, impossible to corral, warming but dangerous, seem an apt image for the powerful and living Mystery we call "God." This Fire reappears in the Gospel, hidden in cloud at the Annunciation (cf. Luke 1:35) and the Ascension (Acts 1:9), and glimpsed briefly by the disciples in Jesus transfigured on the mountain (cf. Matt 17:2). It signifies the Presence of God's all-burning love. It has taken on permanent human reality in Jesus Christ, the light of the world (John 8:12). And it is unquenchable (cf. John 1:4-5).

Eternal rest grant unto our dead, O Lord, and let *this* perpetual light shine upon them!

O Wisdom

O Wisdom,
O Holy Word of God,
you govern all creation with your strong yet tender care.
Come and show your people the way to salvation.

O Sapientia,
quae ex ore Altissimi prodiisti,
attingens a fine usque ad finem, fortiter suaviterque
disponens omnia:
veni ad docendum nos viam prudentiae.

—from the *O Antiphons*

Deep in December, in the final week of Advent, Wisdom remembers as she sits by the Fire and knits. She has a long memory. She is an old woman.

Wisdom was there before the beginning and she saw it all happen—light from darkness, dry land from sea, earth carpeted with green growing things. And she was no mere spectator. She was God's companion artisan, playing with delight in the fields of creation (Proverbs 8). She is in fact the personification of God's creating Word, the logos knitted into the very core of creation, providing it with pattern and coherence (Genesis 1). She is the wise woman who builds herself a house, sets her table, and invites to the feast all those who seek life (Proverbs 9). She reflects the Shepherd turned host in God's house in Psalm 23. Serene, changeless, all-seeing, Wisdom shows us God's face.

Still deeper in December, on Christmas morning, we will recall that the Word, whom Old Testament Wisdom personifies, took on human flesh in Jesus Christ (John 1:14). St. Paul understood. He called Christ "the wisdom of God" (1 Cor 1:24). In Christ, wisdom assumes a human face that reflects the light from the divine countenance sought so assiduously by psalmists (e.g., Ps 67:2). St. Luke tells us that Jesus grew, as we must, "in wisdom" as he grew in age (Luke 2:52).

In us, the members of Christ's Body, humanity continues to grow in wisdom as we remember the very long history of human experience, wisdom's greatest teacher. Wisdom's human face is scarred by thorns, lined with suffering, and marked by the enduring quest to make sense out of a world that often seems to be disintegrating into the chaos that governed before the Word gave it order and purpose.

So Wisdom still sits by the Fire, who is God (cf. Exodus 3), and knits past and present together into meaning and value. And each of us has been entrusted with a portion of the pattern.

O Wisdom, O Holy Word of God, come, teach us how to knit!

Tower of Ivory, Pray for Us!

Mother of our Savior . . .
Mirror of justice,
Seat of wisdom,
Cause of our joy,
Spiritual vessel,
Vessel of honor,
Singular vessel of devotion,
Mystical rose,
Tower of David,
Tower of ivory . . .
Health of the sick,
Refuge of sinners,
Comforter of the afflicted,
Help of Christians . . .
Queen of families,
Queen of peace.
Pray for us.

—from the *Litany of Loreto*

The ivory Madonna stood on each mantelpiece of my child-hood and beyond. I never thought to ask my Southern Methodist father why he had brought her back from an assignment in Africa in 1939, long before importing ivory became illegal (and before we knew the moral gravity of killing endangered animals for capital gain). The Madonna accompanied my father to his bachelor apartment in the San Francisco Bay Area, the first homes he and my mother made together, the home to which he took us in England, and finally to the California house in which he died. She went with my mother then to the Mojave Desert and to Houston. The family surroundings shifted often, but she was always there.

She was silent serenity in the chaos that sometimes threatened to engulf us. She said nothing, and she never changed.

She was veiled and robed in folds of real ivory, warm to the eye, cool to the touch. Her hands were folded in prayer, her rosary beads draped over her left arm, her face almost lit by a smile. She wore an aura of mystery: she knew something I could hardly guess at, and she found her peace there. She was beautiful, and I loved her, even as a small child in a Protestant household.

"Ivory tower" implies withdrawal from the everyday world into irrelevance, but this Madonna never lost her footing in the harsh realities of the world from which she came. She stood on a base that retained the stained brown surface of the tusk from which she had been carved. When my world grew painfully muddied, as the worlds of childhood and youth often do, I knew somehow that she understood.

When I was ten, Marist Sisters introduced me to the *Litany of Loreto.* Most of the words were alien to me, but when we came to "Tower of ivory, pray for us," I recognized our Madonna and was reassured. Even amid the unfamiliarity of an English Catholic school, she was still there.

Slender watchtower of unbreakable strength, serene beacon of beauty in the frenzied ugliness of our world, survivor from faraway places ever present in the streets where we live, pillar of light carved from dark wildness, silent word of prayer amid the incessant chatter of our lives: Tower of ivory, pray for us!

Blessing of Work

O Lord, look with favor upon your servants,
and upon the works of our hands.
"And may the gracious care of the Lord our God be upon us.
Direct the work of our hands for us.
O direct the work of our hands" (Ps 90:17).*

> Glory to the Father, and to the Son, and to the Holy Spirit,
> as it was in the beginning, is now, and will be forever.
> Amen.

Why ask God's blessing on something as mundane as work?

When we watch a mushroom cloud rising above the unbearable ruin of life in Hiroshima and Nagasaki, or the smoke billowing from the crematoria of Auschwitz, we might look toward heaven and ask, "Where were you?" But I wonder, if we listened, whether we would hear God reply: "Where were you?" Hard to deny that the mushroom cloud and the chimney smoke were the work of human hands.

Work was woven into the human fabric from the start. We first see God busy about what Genesis calls the work of creation (Gen 1–2:1). The climax of God's creative work was human beings, created in the image of that very same God. Entrusted with the care of everything just made (Gen 1:28-29) or set in a garden rich in fruit trees (Gen 2:8), the first human beings were also intended to be creative workers, cultivating the future God had built into all living things.

The first explicit human assignment was to pick fruit for food (Gen 2:15-16), presumably to strengthen earth's new cultivators for their task. But before the story got too far, the work went badly astray, thanks to that chat with the serpent (Gen 3:1-7). Instead of expressing human being's true identity and purpose in relation to Creator and creation, labor was twisted into the human pursuit of an illusory self in isolation from God and the world. At that moment, mushroom clouds and smoking chimneys became possible.

Fortunately, few of us spend our workdays inventing weapons of mass destruction or new tools for genocide. Our work's content does matter, of course, but what matters more is what truth it tells about us, what relationships it serves, what fruit it bears. Does it reveal the image of God or a self writ large? Does it weave bonds or tear them asunder? Does it bear the fragrance of fruit trees or the odor of smoke?

O Lord, direct the work of our hands—and our hearts and minds and imaginations. Direct the work of our hands to your own ends, and make those ends ours. Amen.

* The translation of this psalm is from the prayer used in my community, the Abbey of St. Walburga.

Night Prayer for the Sick

Watch, O Lord, with those who wake, or watch, or weep tonight,
and give your Angels and Saints charge over those who sleep.
Tend your sick ones, O Lord Christ.
Rest your weary ones.
Bless your dying ones.
Soothe your suffering ones.
Pity your afflicted ones.
Shield your joyous ones.
And all for your love's sake. Amen.

—St. Augustine

Night creeps into the sickroom armed with all the frightening fantasies that sent us scurrying for a parent's room when we were children. But the fears are not just a trick of the dark. For the sick and those at their bedside, there really is a monster under the bed, but it's all too real, and its name is death.

Come now, you're saying, I only have the flu!

True, perhaps, but when even the least sickness has done a hatchet job on our rational response to the dark, night somehow stirs up the vulnerability our genes remember from the days when human beings cowered in caves unable to ward off predators they couldn't see. What we can see better in the dark than in the daylight, however, is that every sickness is a secret harbinger of our mortality, a silent whisper that one day this very flesh will ultimately betray us. At such times we can feel very small, very scared, and very much alone.

What sign do we have then that Christ hasn't gone home for the night, leaving us to our own pitiful devices? We have words, words of prayer like this one, attributed to St. Augustine. They invoke what we most need: the assurance that Christ never goes home for the night, that he is right there at the bedside, keeping watch over us and our loved ones (cf. Matt

28:20). Where Christ is, love is (cf. 1 John 4:1; Rom 8:35-39). And love is never idle. The Christ of the sickroom is busy tending us, resting us, soothing us, pitying us, and shielding us, whether we are sick, weary, suffering, or even joyful!

This prayer slips into that comforting list a quiet reminder that even when the monster comes out from under the bed for real to carry us away, Christ is there with us, blessing us with the sign of the cross, the sign of life forever triumphant over death. Before that sign, the monster is transformed into a ride across the threshold in Christ's arms, with the angels and saints for company.

Whether we are sick in bed or keeping vigil at the bedside, we may not feel the comfort, but deep in the bones of our being, we somehow know that the love this prayer calls on is the Light hidden and unquenchable in every darkness (cf. John 1:3-5)

A Prayer for All Seasons

Lord have mercy.
Thee I adore.
Into Thy hands.

—Elizabeth Goudge

In Elizabeth Goudge's novel *The Scent of Water,* an elderly clergyman—a man with a tenuous hold on sanity and sobriety but a profound grasp of the wisdom learned from suffering—teaches the above prayer to a desperate young woman long besieged by bouts of crippling depression. "My dear," he says, "love, your God, is a trinity. There are three necessary prayers and they have three words each. They are these: 'Lord have mercy. Thee I adore. Into Thy hands.' Not difficult to remember. If in times of distress you hold to these you will do well."

Since I read the novel years ago, this triplet has become my favorite "connector" prayer in good times and in bad. When I have become unmoored from the Center amid the clamoring demands of my daily life—the tug of too many things on my task list, the interruption of knocks on my office door, the intrusions of the monastery intercom bells announcing that I have a phone call, or just the thoughts that buzz around uninvited in my ever-busy brain—the words reconnect me. It's a simple "You are" and "I am" prayer that rejoins the "I" with the "You." It recalls me to the essential fact that wherever my mind has gone, my feet are firmly planted in the present moment, and my present moment has a name: Jesus Christ.

Tradition abounds with these little connector prayers: St. Thomas's famous, "My Lord and my God!" (John 20:28); the Eastern Jesus Prayer, "Lord Jesus Christ, Son of God, have mercy on me, a sinner"; the psalmist's "O God, come to my assistance; / O Lord, make haste to help me!" (Ps 70:2); the "Jesus, Mary, and Joseph" or "Sacred Heart of Jesus, have mercy on us" taught me by the Irish school Sisters of my youth. These connectors are legion. When I entered the convent in 1965, in my pre-Benedictine days, I found many of them listed in our pocket-sized *Manual of Prayers*. Some were even assigned to specific activities. But they were many and soon forgotten when I left the novitiate for the classroom. As the old clergyman predicted, Elizabeth Goudge's little prayer has proven unforgettable in its simplicity.

"Pray without ceasing," wrote St. Paul (1 Thess 5:17). And he made the point again and again (e.g., Rom 12:12; Eph 5:20; Phil 4:6; Col 4:2). Of course he was echoing Jesus on "the necessity . . . to pray always without becoming weary" (Luke 18:1) We Christians have long known that when in our busy distractions we cut the umbilical cord of prayer that joins us to God, we are cut off from the essential source of our life and find ourselves stunted, incomplete, and dissatisfied. But experience, like a splash of cold water, forces us to face practical reality. We live on the ground, not in some attractive ethereal cloud. Ceaseless prayer seems like a mountain too high, a bridge too far. Our elders in wisdom have always come to our rescue, like the old clergyman in Goudge's novel. If you want to grow into unceasing prayer, they teach us, start here, start now, and start small. Find simple words and weave a cord with them: hold onto your end, and God will hold onto the other. The methods are many. The custom of the "prayer word" in centering prayer, the murmured phrases from *lectio divina*, even the *Liturgy of the Hours* grew out of this principle.

As a Benedictine, I do indeed practice daily *lectio divina*. I pray the *Liturgy of the Hours* at fixed times in order to learn to pray at all times, as early Church theory proposed. But when push comes to shove, as it often does, I press the pause button and just pray, "Lord have mercy. Thee I adore. Into Thy hands." And the threatened life cord is secured once again.

Why not try it?

Lamb of God: A Prayer of Fragments

Lamb of God, you take away the sins of the world, have mercy on us.
Lamb of God, you take away the sins of the world, have mercy on us.
Lamb of God, you take away the sins of the world, grant us peace.

In the 2014 movie *Son of God*, Jesus tears a large flat "loaf" of bread into pieces and passes them around the table to his disciples. The tearing hurts to see, followed as it is by the words, "This is my Body, given for you." It makes me re-envision the moment when Jesus takes a basket of loaves, the thick barley bread of the poor, and tears them for distribution among the hungry crowd (Mark 6:34-44). I see in my mind's eye the raw, uneven edges of the fragments, the scattered crumbs, the rough texture of the bread. Tearing seems more powerful than the clean, impersonal, painless breaking up of crisp, identical machine-made hosts that happens on most of our altars at the Eucharistic celebration.

But in the Eucharist we personalize it. We give the bread a title now synonymous with the name Jesus: Lamb of God. The title, given to Jesus by John the Baptist (John 1:29), is haunted by the memory of real lambs subjected to the butcher's knife in Egypt on that terrible night when the their blood, sprinkled on door posts, was the only thing that stood between the Israelites and the Angel of Death passing over in the night (Exodus 12). The paschal lamb died so the firstborn, the people's cherished future, could live. And so did Jesus die, his blood staining the wood of the cross as he suffered to guarantee not one nation's future but the future of the entire human race. Our future. Nothing clean, impersonal, or painless about that.

And nothing as cost-and-effort free as a parish-provided bag of hosts seems to us in the pews. The Lamb of God, hanging torn and bleeding, pays with his life to take away the sins of the world. Our sins. The sins of selfishness by which we tear the bonds of human love to pieces. They sometimes sound so small, those sins, when we trot them out in the confessional, maybe even without embarrassment, for simple, clean removal accomplished by a few words of absolution. We forget how our sins dig into us, twist us away from our truth, tear us away from the loving communion with God and one another that is our destiny, and leave us broken fragments of Christ's Body, the one, new undivided humanity (cf. Eph 2:14-15). We come as fragments to communion to receive the fragments of the living Bread by which all the fragments are made one (1 Cor 10:16-17).

We pray to the Lamb of God for mercy before we step out into the aisle. I wonder how often we think of mercy as an act of a God who stands over there, maybe up there before us, and pronounces words of forgiveness over us or gives us "something." I wonder how often we realize that the Lamb of God *is* the mercy who has come to us in living Eucharistic flesh and blood, in holy bread and cup, as he came at the Incarnation.

The prophet Micah provides the clue to this mystery of mercy. We pray to the Lamb for peace, but the prophet promised more: the One to come would not simply give us peace. Rather, he *is* our peace, the One who gathers up the broken fragments and makes them whole (Mic 5:4; cf. Eph 2:14).

The Eucharist is the Church's school of prayer. So who says that we, fragmented as we sometimes become in the wrangling of daily life, cannot stop at any moment and pray the prayer we have learned there: "Lamb of God, you take away the sins of the world, have mercy on us and grant us peace. Oh, grant us peace!"

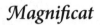

Magnificat

My soul proclaims the greatness of the Lord,
my spirit rejoices in God my Savior
for he has looked with favor on his lowly servant. . . .
He has shown the strength of his arm,
he has scattered the proud in their conceit.
He has cast down the mighty from their thrones,
and has lifted up the lowly.
He has filled the hungry with good things,
and the rich he has sent away empty.

The song that overflows from Mary's unexpected experience of becoming the mother of the "Son of the Most High" has rippled through Christian prayer ever since. The Church prays it every evening in the *Liturgy of the Hours*.

In its Gospel context Mary comes to her aging cousin Elizabeth and to us bearing Good News: the child in her womb and the song on her lips (Luke 1:39-45). In the verses above the words fall like dew on the parched lives of those victimized by others' pride and conceit and of those starved by others' greed.

But what about us when we can't number ourselves among the lowly? What about the days when our autobiography records the nasty little satisfaction of seeing another person green with jealousy because of the award or raise or grade we got and they did not? What about the times when memory confronts us with the evening we splurged at the restaurant and left a meager tip for the lean-looking waiter, to say nothing of the table bussers with children to feed, because we'd spent extra on the wine? These may not be your stories, but what about the others that are? Is there no good news for the likes of us who are blinded by selfish illusions of superiority and power?

God is not so stingy. Mary sings of the Mercy that brings good tidings to everyone. But she warns that it will cost us. We will be "scattered" in our conceit, even if it's only about a straighter nose or a more fashionable wardrobe or our children's school grades. We will have to fumble in the confusion of goals lost and priorities rearranged. We will be knocked off our high horse, the one from which we worked so hard to control our little kingdom—even if it was just the matter of controlling a spouse's eating habits or a teenager's chaotic room. We will find ourselves hungry as we're required to give up feasting at the cost of others' famine. All the habits of conceit, pride, and extravagant consumption at others' expense— and our own—will have to go, no matter how insignificant we thought them. And no matter where we stand on the social ladder or the affluence scale.

The Good News that Mary bears in her womb and in her words has in fact come to strip all of us of those straitjackets of heart we've learned to wear, so that we can stand among those whom Christ has set free of the burdens of imagined thrones, crowns, and scepters. That won't sound like Good News while we're wrestling with the choices it requires, but it's the best news there is because the last burden to be shed is the death of the heart deformed by our sins (cf. 1 Cor 15:26).

When we who are conceited, proud, or power hungry—even in little ways—change sides in the picture Mary paints, then we too can sing with her, "My spirit rejoices in God my Savior!"

Sorrowful Mysteries of the Rosary

The agony in the garden
The scourging at the pillar
The crowning with thorns
The carrying of the cross
The crucifixion

As I look back on my mother's long, slow walk through aging, dementia, and death, I am struck by how completely she was stripped of everything that she had once considered essential. She was widowed in her forties. In subsequent years, her children left home one by one, and her financial security dwindled. In her seventies, unable to manage on her own, she was forced to abandon the cherished independence of her longtime home for a small house nearer her children. Growing dementia sent her first to assisted living and finally to a nursing home, where she was stripped of her all-important solitude and given a roommate. Coherent speech deserted her, this lifelong entertaining conversationalist; her legs forgot how to walk; and the family who visited her several times a week became puzzling strangers with no names. And finally, peacefully, she lost her last breath to emphysema. She let it all go without complaint.

The sorrowful mysteries of the rosary lay out just such a pattern of progressive stripping and loss. In the agony of the garden, Jesus is gradually stripped of his greatest supporters, his disciples. Even Peter, James, and John fall asleep repeatedly; Jesus' vigil is interrupted by the arrival of the betrayer, the first of the disciples to leave him, and followed by the desertion of all the rest (Matt 26:40-45, 57; Mark 14:37-41, 50; Luke 23:47). His torturers scourge him at the pillar and strip him of all vestiges of human dignity, numbering this respected if controversial rabbi among criminals. The soldiers strip him of his garments and clothe him in the mockery of a purple cloak and crown of thorns (Matt 27: 26-31; Mark 15:15-20; John 19:1-3). This strong young laborer, who had walked the roads of Palestine indefatigably for three years, is now so weakened by sleep deprivation and blood loss that he must accept the help of strangers to carry his cross (Matt 27:32; Mark 15:21; Luke 23:26). And, even so, he falls under its weight, an episode reported in the stations of the cross, though not in the Gospels. At Calvary, the soldiers take his clothing away and cast lots for it, like spoils of conquest (Matt 27:35; Mark 15:24; Luke 23:34; John 19:23-24). The King, whose kingdom is not of this world, is defeated. On the cross, Jesus loses all that remains to him. The jeering crowd—so different from those who once eagerly sought him out—casts doubt on his very life's purpose (Matt 27:39-44; Mark 15:29-32; Luke 23:35-37). Surely, they say, one can see that he has failed in his mission. Having seemingly lost even the sustaining presence of his Father, Jesus gives up his very life's breath (Matt 27:46; Mark 15:34).

This story of stripping and loss is our story too. But it does not await us simply at the end of the road. Jesus tells us to take up our cross daily and follow him—where else but through that lifelong process of abandoning everything, even our very selves (Matt 10:38-39; Mark 7:24-25; Luke 9:23-25)? Along the way, he tells us to leave behind homes, loved ones, property, status, power—all those treasures we spend so much of our lives accumulating and then clinging to for dear life. We may not be called to leave them all literally—often quite the contrary—but we are called to hold them lightly so we can share them readily when the service of God's reign requires it. Others first, not self first, is a law that requires a lot of dying if we would really live into it. In the sorrowful mysteries, Jesus shows us how.

And he began the stripping of his passion before the sorrowful mysteries pick up the story. At the Last Supper, he stripped off his garments and donned a towel, the garment of a slave, to wash the disciples' feet (John 13:1-11). Even further back, at the incarnation, he stripped off his glory in order to join our enslaved humanity and free us from the power of sin and death (Phil 2:6-8).

And at the end of our earthly life, when we are stripped of all that has kept us stunted, Christ will meet us and reclothe us in himself, who wears now the robe of his risen glory (cf. Gal 3:27). This is the mystery we celebrate at every Eucharist, when all dying becomes life.

Psalm 24: The Meeting

Who shall climb the mountain of the LORD?
Who shall stand in his holy place?
The clean of hands and pure of heart,
whose soul is not set on vain things,
who has not sworn deceitful words. (vv. 3-4)

Psalm 24 tells the story of a meeting about to happen. The appointed place is the temple atop Mount Zion in Jerusalem. There are two on the way to the meeting: a pilgrim—who represents all those "who seek the face of the God of Jacob" (v. 6)—and the very God of Jacob.

As our story opens, the pilgrim is toiling up the hill toward the temple. The climber must be a daring character. Whatever the angle of the road, the criteria for climbing it are steep: "The clean of hands and pure of heart, / whose soul is not set on vain things, / who has not sworn deceitful words."

In the biblical world, clean hands are not merely the product of a thorough scrub with soap and water. The phrase often means hands specifically not stained with blood. As King David of old journeyed toward Jerusalem, Shimei (a member of the clan of Saul, whom David defeated in battle and replaced as king) curses David as a "man of blood" (2 Sam 16:7-8). But the blood that stains David's hands most memorably is the blood of Uriah the Hittite, whose death David connived to bring about so that he could marry Uriah's wife, Bathsheba, already carrying David's child.

I am reminded of the famous sleepwalking scene in Shakespeare's play *Macbeth*. Lady Macbeth, guilt-ridden after goading her husband into making a bid for kingship by murdering Scotland's king Duncan in his sleep, tries in vain to scrub the stain of Duncan's blood off her own hands, crying, "Out, damned spot. . . . What, will these hands ne'er be clean? . . . Here's the smell of the blood still."

Unlike Lady Macbeth, King David has done sincere penance for his sin and has been forgiven by God, but the smell of Uriah's blood forever lingers about his name. That meaning of clean hands always loiters in the biblical background, for murder is the epitome of doing harm to another. But "clean of hands" eventually took on a broader meaning. It came to mean for the psalmist one who is free of the stain of any kind of wrong done to another. Who can claim that kind of spotlessness?

The most difficult of the demands laid upon the would-be climber, though, is not clean hands but a pure heart. Purity of heart is a term with a very long history in biblical and later Christian spirituality. The nineteenth-century Danish philosopher Søren Kierkegaard defined it very simply as "to will one thing." In Scripture, the pure heart is the heart set on God alone. Only the pure of heart can "see the face of God" (cf. Matt 5:8). Russian author Leo Tolstoy tells a powerful story that illustrates purity of heart. In "The Three Hermits" (1886), a bishop visits three old hermits who live alone on a remote island. They know no set prayers, so he teaches them the "Our Father." When they seem to have learned it thoroughly, the bishop sets sail in the ship that landed him on the island, but during the night, to the sailors' terror and the bishop's wonder, the three old hermits are seen running across the water after the boat. When they catch up with it, they explain to the bishop that they had forgotten the words he had taught them and had run after him to ask him to teach them again. So intent were they on the prayer, they did not notice that they had been running across the sea. That is the heart fixed only on God!

The psalmist adds more details. The pure heart has no room for vain desires or deceitful words (v. 4). The heart fixed on God loses interest in goods we sometimes collect so diligently, though they're nothing but empty husks that feed our vanity or our fear of empty hours. The heart fixed on God also forgets the varied vocabulary of falsehood, even the "little white lie." How could deceptions be of any interest to the climber who has in his or her sights only the God who is truth (cf. 1 John 5:6)?

Besides the stiff criteria for approaching the temple, there is another reason the climbers would need courage: they are about to meet "the king of glory" (vv. 7-10). And who is this king? "The LORD, the mighty, the valiant; / the LORD, the valiant in war" (v. 8). This is no less than "the LORD of hosts" (v. 10), resplendent in the fiery cloud biblical writers call "the glory of God." So great is this divine Hero that the temple gates, already impressive in height, must stretch even taller to admit the awesome figure (v. 9). Annie Dillard famously makes this point when she writes that if we had any idea how awesome God is, we would wear "crash helmets" to church on Sunday and ushers would "issue life preservers and signal

flares"! The climber of old, suggests the psalmist, might want
to take similar precautions before heading up to that meeting.
Nevertheless, despite demand and danger, the reward is worth
the dare, says the psalmist. "Blessings from the LORD shall [the
pilgrim] receive, / and right reward from the God who saves
him" (v. 5).

The psalmist leaves us holding our breath: what will happen
when this admirable human being comes face to face with this
glory-clad God? We never find out. The psalmist walks away,
with the scene set, but the story unfinished.

Jesus finishes it for us in Luke 18:10-14. He tells us a story
about two pilgrims who went up to the temple one fine day to
pray. The first, a Pharisee, steps immediately to the forefront
of attention. As far as he is concerned, he has certainly met
the psalmist's criteria for one who can dare to climb the Lord's
mountain and stand in the holy place. He is purer minded
than most, thinking only of the precepts of the law. He obeys
them scrupulously. He does not set his soul on such vain
things as his wallet or his dinner. On the contrary, he fasts
twice a week and pays tithes on all he has earned. Lest someone should begin to inquire about what he eats on the other
five days of the week or about how he came by the money he
pays tithes with, he hastens to say that he is not greedy or
dishonest under any circumstances. He is not even adulterous.
No, he is as pure as the driven snow on a cold Jerusalem day
in winter. He marches right up to the front of the temple area
and puts all these holy credentials into a resume he reads out
as a prayer. And, to be honest, it is a very impressive list of
right things done and wrong things avoided. He is indeed, as
he claims to be, not like the rest of humanity—meaning us.

Perhaps it is merely an accident of English translation that
the text says the Pharisee "spoke this prayer to himself." Maybe
Jesus intends only to tell us that at least he didn't trumpet his
perfections out loud. But the English is apt. And true. The

Pharisee may very well want to impress the Divine Listener, but he is obviously far too taken up with himself to get beyond the borders of his own ego. Or perhaps, since he knows he is "not like the rest of humanity," he preens himself before a different mirror than the rest of us. "See, the image of God!" he might say, looking at the God he has painted in his mind, the one who will surely pat his back and call him blessed.

And God's reply? There is none. Or perhaps none the Pharisee can hear. God's love may surround the ego-wrapped human spirit with fiery fidelity (cf. Zech 2:9), but God will not breach the walls. Notice that the risen Christ walks through locked doors but not through locked hearts (John 20:19, 24-29). Perhaps the greatest of this law-abiding Pharisee's tragedies is that he doesn't even notice God knocking.

We ought not be too quick to criticize though. Most of us couldn't even be there, according to the psalmist. The requirements for the climber would daunt the stoutest of hearts. It takes a lifetime to grow into purity of heart, if we ever do this side of the grave. How, then, would we dare to climb the hill to the temple as the pilgrim does, as the Pharisee has? Guiltless of any harm done to another? Totally focused on God and therefore God's will? No tiny white lies? No history of straying off the path to explore some tempting byway or chase some attractive mirage or take a nap in a nearby poppy field? No, we are the rest of humanity, we wanderers from the straight and narrow road, we sin-pocked of heart, we fragile and flawed human beings.

But the second pilgrim in Jesus' story gives us hope. He is a tax collector, which makes him a sinner by definition. Tax collectors in first-century Palestine collaborated with the Roman occupation government. They contracted to collect whatever taxes the Roman civic and military leaders set, with the understanding that they were free to line their own pockets with whatever they could extort over and above what they had contracted to pay to their Roman employers. The law-abiding Pharisees despised them, as does the Pharisee in the story, who prides himself on being in every way unlike this tax collector. Yet the tax collector, guilty of putting his compatriots in financial jeopardy, valuing his personal wealth above his neighbors' well-being, dirtying his hands with Roman money, and seeking his own comfort rather than service of God according to the law, has climbed the temple hill regardless of the fact that he meets none of the psalmist's criteria.

How did he dare? Perhaps instead of Psalm 24, he has prayed a different psalm, one the Pharisee would never need to pray. In Psalm 51, ascribed to the penitent David after his double sin of adultery and murder, the psalmist owns guilt without reservation: "O see, in guilt I was born, / a sinner when my mother conceived me" (v. 7). Yet this psalmist believes that the impure heart is not incurable. Instead, he prays, "Cleanse me with hyssop, and I shall be pure; / wash me, and I shall be whiter than snow" (v. 9) and "Create a pure heart for me, O God . . ." (v. 12). Rather than remain at the bottom of the hill, not daring to approach God, the tax collector makes it up to the temple and into the Divine Presence intending only to beg, as this psalmist does, "Do not cast me away from your presence" (v. 13). With Psalm 51 on the lips, even the tax collector can dare the climb to the meeting at the temple.

Psalm 24 may describe the God who will meet the pilgrims as the warrior "king of glory," and "Lord of hosts" (v. 10), indeed the creator of the universe (vv. 1-2), but the Pharisee and the tax collector bring two very different images of God to the meeting with them. The Pharisee seems to have recast God in his own image. Jesus describes that image vividly on another occasion: "Woe to you, scribes and Pharisees, you hypocrites. You pay tithes of mint and dill and cummin, and have neglected the weightier things of the law: judgment and mercy and fidelity" (Matt 23:23). The Pharisee in the story plainly expects the God he serves to applaud him for the tithes of mint and dill and cummin, the fasts and the truth telling. Equally plainly the Pharisee gives no thought at all to the divine mercy because he has no need of it.

The tax collector, on the other hand, out of the depths of his own sinful misery, thinks of nothing else. His prayer, empty of any hint of self-congratulation, is short and simple: "O God, be merciful to me a sinner." And it is the God of mercy he hopes will hear him.

There were two prayers said in the temple that day. But only one of them was answered. It is the tax collector, says Jesus, not the Pharisee who went home justified because God *is* mercy.

Psalm 81: God in the Storm

A voice I did not know said to me:
"I freed your shoulder from the burden;
You called in distress and I delivered you.
I answered, concealed in the thunder." (vv. 6c, 7a, 8ab)

Human beings are born seekers. The mandate to "seek God" runs like a silver thread throughout the Scriptures. Benedictines have pondered deeply what it means to "seek God in all things" (cf. *Rule of St. Benedict*, 58:7). The phrase occurs in a short list of criteria Benedict provides for judging the authenticity of a novice's vocation. The last criterion on the list is the stumbling block for most of us: does this novice "show eagerness" for trials? The phrase is variously translated and interpreted, but it identifies the stumbling block that causes many of us to fall flat on our faces in our efforts to "seek God in all things"—it's suffering.

When the storm cloud of suffering settles round us, then the seeking becomes most difficult. How can we seek God when we have the pressing issue of pain on our minds? The chaos blinds and deafens us. We flounder, unable to find the path on which we walked with such confidence yesterday. We cry out for deliverance. At such times, we remember the story of Jesus stilling the storm, once the disciples succeeded in waking him up (Matt 8:23-27). Perhaps if we pray louder, we can wake God up and get this storm taken care of so we can get on with the business of seeking God. What kind of protest, cajolery, or bribe will stir Jesus out of his irritating sleep? What will it take to get him up and moving? Maybe if we promise to give up smoking or late-night TV . . . maybe if we promise to be kind to that irksome neighbor or to listen to that deadening bore . . . maybe if we promise to make nine novenas . . . maybe . . . Maybe we should stop looking for our own solutions and listen.

In a minute. Okay, if God is not going to still this storm, let's ask for deliverance of a different kind. Meaninglessness is intolerable to the human spirit. To find something meaningless is either to find no explanation for it or to find no purpose for it.

The suffering would not be so bad if we could understand the reason for it. Often, in fact, the first form of deliverance we ask for is an explanation: "Why are you letting this happen? Why me? Why now?" What we really want is self-justification from the all-powerful but not, at the moment, all-merciful Providence. We are Job, challenging God to defend himself before the bar of our human notion of justice. However, if God is silent, we often scurry after a scapegoat. If my coworker hadn't given me that cold . . . if my superiors had understood that I was overworked . . . if the school staff had paid more attention to my child . . . if terrorists had left the World Trade Center alone so we wouldn't be tempted to go to war . . . if it hadn't been a full moon. Casting the blame on someone or something else—even our silent God—does nothing to still the storm, but it does sometimes make it more bearable because it provides some sort of indirect rationale for the trouble. It also absolves us of any responsibility. That matters because our last recourse, if no other explanation is forthcoming, is to probe our own shortcomings. If I had lost weight . . . if I hadn't gone out of town just then . . . if I had paid more attention . . . if I hadn't irritated my boss . . .

If no explanation is forthcoming from any quarter, we may then turn to the task of finding a purpose for it all. Here the "comforts of religion" can be a poor excuse for evading God. Many of us were taught, when faced with pain, to "offer it up"—usually meaning that we should use it as intercessory prayer or gift for someone else's need. That is an admirable ideal when, in fact, we have plumbed the pain to its depth. In the hands of saints, it is a powerful tool for good. However, when we are simply looking for a way out, it's a cheap exit. It invites a kind of resignation that is often a thin veil for passive-aggressive resentment. Muttered behind our hands joined in prayer are whispers of, "Okay, God, look, I'm offering it up, aren't you going to do something? At least console me for my piety? At least let me know that I've sprung someone from purgatory or made my child go back to the sacraments!" This is mere bargaining in disguise. Bargaining is a normal stage in the grief process, but it's healthier if we call it what it is.

The introduction to the Church's rites for the sick and dying urges the sick to unite their sufferings with Christ's (cf. Rom 8:17) for "the welfare of the people of God" (no. 5). That's actually the theological point implicit in the notion of offering something up—we make our offering in communion with Christ's self-offering on the cross for all those whom he has redeemed by his suffering and death. The goal is not to eliminate the suffering by baptizing it with religious language. Communion with Christ on the cross includes communion with the One who cried out in absolute darkness of soul, "My God, my God, why have you forsaken me?" This is the food of highest holiness through truly redemptive suffering, but it's not for the fainthearted seeking an escape from the unbearable.

In the end, when we've run out of solutions of our own, perhaps we must finally stop and listen. There is a point at which, brought to our knees, we must abandon the search for deliverance and, instead, seek God. Up until now, we have been seeking not God but something from God: escape, explanation, purpose. Those are all natural, normal, healthy responses to suffering. And, in fact, we are unlikely to give them up. However, we might pause for a moment and come to rest before the stark fact that the Benedictine mandate—not reserved only to Benedictines—is to seek God in all things. *All* things. Not just the joyful things. Not just the pleasant things. Not just the reasonable things. All things. All things include the storm cloud. If we are truly to seek God, without a shred of our own well-being disguised in the search, we must at some point seek God with no strings attached.

The psalmist has captured both dilemma and grace: "You called in distress and I delivered you. / I answered, concealed in the thunder." We may not recognize the salvation. We may not hear the answer. We may not see the storm cloud swirl aside, even for a moment, so that we can glimpse the face of God. Nevertheless, in the darkness of faith, we reach out and touch God in the irreplaceable split second when the heart knows beyond doubt that we have found the one we seek. It changes nothing: the suffering closes over us again. It changes everything: we who suffer will never be the same again. As Job discovered in his moment of truth, it is enough (Job 38-41).

And it is gift, not achievement. All we can do is lay aside our frantic quest for our own fix and, in the poverty and nakedness of faith, stand before God's door and knock. It will, we have been promised, open (Matt 7:7).

Psalm 121: Travel Prayer

I lift up my eyes to the mountains;
from where shall come my help?
My help shall come from the LORD,
who made heaven and earth.

He will keep your foot from stumbling.
Your guard will never slumber.
No, he sleeps not nor slumbers,
Israel's guard.

The LORD your guard, the LORD your shade
at your right hand.
By day the sun shall not smite you,
nor the moon in the night.

The LORD will guard you from evil;
he will guard your soul.
The LORD will guard your going and coming,
both now and forever.

We are a traveling people. Work, play, or simply itchy feet, all seem to keep us often on the road or in the air. Summer in particular releases many of us from the thrall of school, job, or winter's ice and snow to go farther than the grocery store or the classroom or the workplace in search of recreation, rest, family time, alone time, or the novelty of distant places.

But all travel has its hazards, as the author of this biblical travel prayer knew very well. We know the practical precautions: be watchful, take sunscreen, protect your identity documents. The psalmist takes a deeper look.

Wary or asleep, we never go unprotected because we never go alone, night or day, the psalmist reminds us, because our God never sleeps. We might need to clear away a little brush to find this truth reassuring: this God is not the ever-present Judge, taking note of every wrongful thought or deed in a little black book for use against us in the end. This is the God who is love (1 John 4:16), love that takes no vacation from working in every way, imaginable and unimaginable, to bring us to life at its fullest (cf. John 10:10)—whether in the car, on the plane, at the beach, mosquito bitten, pickpocketed, lost, or safe at home.

We can take sunscreen, but God in Christ steps between us and every fiery dart from evil's bow, as the Letter to the Ephesians would say (cf. Eph 6:16). It helps to recognize that the sun and moon were considered gods by some of Israel's polytheistic neighbors and as such shed deceptive light, tempting God's people onto harmful paths.

We can protect our identity documents, but God, who made us in the divine image (Gen 1:27) and wove us into Christ's Body (e.g., 1 Cor 12:12), protects our inmost truth.

We can even hire bodyguards, but God guards our deepest selves, our souls, from every form of evil awaiting us on the road (e.g., Ps 57:7; 140:6).

The kicker is that this God never goes off duty. Night and day, as we leave and as we return, we are always under the protection of Love in all its creative inventiveness and abiding strength, greater than the strength of mountains.

So, take whatever you need for your trip, but pack Psalm121 in your pocket. Take it out and read it along the way. Read it at home, for that matter. It contains the one promise that will never be broken: God's love is with us always (Matt 28:20).

Psalm 130: Prayer for the Dead (De Profundis)

Out of the depths I cry to you, O LORD;
Lord, hear my voice!
O let your ears be attentive
to the sound of my pleadings.

If you, O LORD, should mark iniquities,
Lord, who could stand?
But with you is found forgiveness,
that you may be revered.

I long for you, O LORD,
my soul longs for his word.
My soul hopes in the Lord
more than watchmen for daybreak.

More than watchmen for daybreak,
let Israel hope for the Lord.
For with the Lord there is mercy,
in him is plentiful redemption.
It is he who will redeem Israel
from all its iniquities.

We know the fear but not the facts. The territory beyond death lies unexplored by anyone still living. From this side of the grave, we can be sure that many of us, perhaps even most of us, will walk through that last door unprepared for the destination for which we hope. A life entirely saturated in love? Me? Not hardly!

For those of us not yet ready for that best ending but not deserving of the worst, the Church has hammered out hope of a time, the outer edge of time between death and eternity, when we can become prepared. The one fact we know about that interval—and this only with the surety of faith—is that it will be a time of purification to strip us of every shred of the selfishness that stands between us and that eternal dynamic of love received and returned.

Dissatisfied with abstractions, the Christian imagination has busied itself writing scenarios of the afterlife in which fire looms large. After all, as the Scriptures remind us, fire is the great purifier. But that imagery does nothing to lessen our fears, and so we cry out to God for help. For centuries, the Church has placed on the lips of mourners the *De Profundis*, Latin for the opening of Psalm 130: "Out of the depths." We pray these words for the dead who are still en route between the casket and what lies at journey's final end.

Imagination is at work here too. The psalmists had no thought of future fire. Rather, they often pictured death as the abyss, the pit, the place where the primal waters of chaos roiled in darkness and timelessness. From that water, the Voice of God drew forth everything we know, including human beings (cf. Gen 1:1-2). But the psalmists never got over the fear that the waters would return and sweep us back, dissolving our carefully wrought and tended self into the original broth of unrealized possibilities from which we would not again emerge. No doubt they had observed what the sea did to those it claimed. So they captured their fears in vivid pleas for deliverance. Psalm 130 sits on the beach as the waves creep up, crying out a hope built on God our Rock, not on the sands of our mortality.

The fears may at root be ours, but we dread the thought that these same fears may be stalking those who have gone before us into the pit and long to move beyond it. So, at funerals and in prayers for the dead, we pray Psalm 130 in their name and for their sake.

Out of the lightless depths where the shadow of death falls heavily, we *all* cry to you, O God! Break upon us as the dawn of the day we long to see!

ThisDays Give Us ®

Many of these essays by Sr. Genevieve Glen, OSB, are reflections that first appeared in *Give Us This Day*, a personal daily prayer book published monthly by Liturgical Press.

For more information or to request a sample copy of *Give Us This Day*, go to www.gutd.net or call 888-259-8470.

Also available from *Give Us This Day* Books:

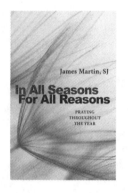

In All Seasons, For All Reasons
Praying Throughout the Year
By James Martin, SJ

Paperback, 84 pp.
$7.95   978-0-8146-4507-9
eBook $4.99   978-0-8146-4531-4

". . . the soul desperately desires to experience this God of love and relationship that Martin writes about."
        —Alex Blechle, *Pray Tell* at praytellblog.com

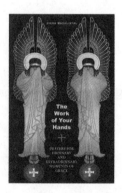

The Work of Your Hands
*Prayers for Ordinary and
Extraordinary Moments of Grace*
by Diana Macalintal

Paperback, 80 pp.
$7.95   978-0-8146-3803-3
eBook $5.99   978-0-8146-3828-6

". . . full of comforting, wise, and useful words that will console and enliven you, and help you do the same for others."
        —Fran Rossi Szpylczyn, *There Will Be Bread*
        at breadhere.wordpress.com

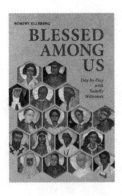